JOINING
CHILDREN
ON THE
SPIRITUAL
JOURNEY

A
BRIDGEPOINT
BOOK

BridgePoint,
an imprint of
Baker Books,
is your connection
for the best in
serious reading
that integrates
the passion of
the heart with
the scholarship
of the mind.

JOINING CHILDREN ON THE SPIRITUAL JOURNEY

NURTURING A LIFE OF FAITH

CATHERINE STONEHOUSE

A BridgePoint Book

A Division of Baker Book House Co
Grand Rapids, Michigan 49516

Published by BridgePoint Books
an imprint of Baker Books
a division of Baker Book House Company
P.O. Box 6287, Grand Rapids, MI 49516-6287

Printed in the United States of America

Library of Congress Cataloging-in-Publication Data

Stonehouse, Catherine.
 Joining children on the spiritual journey : nurturing a life of faith / Catherine Stonehouse.
    p.   cm.
 "A BridgePoint book."
 Includes bibliographical references and index.
 ISBN 0-8010-5807-4 (pbk.)
 1. Christian education of children. I. Title.
BV1475.2.S776   1998
268'.432—dc21   97-48468

Scripture quotations are taken from the New Revised Standard Version of the Bible, copyright 1989 by the Division of Christian Education of the National Council of the Churches of Christ in the USA. Used by permission.

For current information about all releases from Baker Book House, visit our web site:
http://www.bakerbooks.com

To

Tammy, Ted, Paul, and David,
Christie, Julie, and Kara,
my nieces and nephews who
invited me into their
childhood and created for me
the pleasant memories
of their becoming, which illustrate this book,
and who continue to give me the treasured gift of their love.

95106

CONTENTS

ACKNOWLEDGMENTS

My thanks to the many young friends who gave me permission to tell their stories in these pages.

Also, my appreciation to Ellen Dennison, the first "critical" and encouraging reader for each chapter, Dorothy Pohl, an excellent copy editor, and Melinda Van Engen and Lois Stück, skilled editors who helped me polish the manuscript. And thanks to Brenda Story for checking all those footnotes and to acquisitions editor Robert Hosack, who guided the whole project with vision. What a joy to work with each of them.

One

PREPARING
FOR THE JOURNEY

Sarah's parents and grandparents stood before the pastor, and the whole congregation stood behind them, pledging our support to this young family. The pastor held Sarah in his arms as he prayed, "May Sarah Jane become a woman of God." My heart responded, "Yes, Lord." Later I wondered how that would happen. How could we as members of Sarah's church contribute to the answering of that prayer? What did Sarah need from us? What did her parents need? How could we know?

Most churches minister with children in some way. Too often, they simply perpetuate what they have done for many years without questioning whether or not those approaches are effective in forming the faith of children. Some children's workers invest great energy in providing creative, interesting programs. But do they have a reason for the activities that goes beyond holding the children's interest? Do they understand how a child's faith forms and how adults on the spiritual journey with children can most significantly enhance the child's spiritual development?

Spiritual formation during childhood is too important to simply perpetuate programs and hope for the best; it is too important to experiment with approaches without having a way to judge their effectiveness. Parents and those leading children's ministries will be able to facilitate more effectively the spiritual growth of children in their care when they understand the process of spiritual formation.

Christian bookstores are full of books and curriculum resources for use with children. Shelves hold not one but several choices of materials for Sunday school, midweek clubs, vacation Bible school, children's worship, and divorce recovery packaged between colorful covers or in activity boxes. What more does the parent or children's ministry leader need, you may ask.

Let me answer with an illustration: On my desk sits a notebook computer with great potential. A few years ago this technological wonder was the major frustration in my life as I tried to learn a new program and make the computer perform at my command. Now I have mastered the methods for using it to write letters or books and to make transparencies, and most of the time it is no longer a frustration. But the other day a message appeared on the screen: "Major disc error." I was helpless. You see, I know nothing about the inner workings of the computer and, as a result, have no idea how to go about solving major problems. My limited computer knowledge also means that I tap only a fraction of my computer's potential.

Adults who care about children need to understand the inner workings of the developing child. If we do not understand those processes, we will not know when our methods are not contributing to spiritual growth. We will not be able to identify the missing pieces in the child's experience or know how to compensate for the lack. When we understand the process, we will be aware of ways to release the faith community's potential to foster the spiritual life of children. This book is written to lead us in an examination of the inner workings of development and spiritual formation during childhood.

METHODS FOR BUILDING UNDERSTANDING

Where can we turn for an understanding of how faith forms and what experiences children need on their spiritual journey? Where can we find guidelines for the development of ministries with children? People search for such direction in a variety of ways. Four approaches often used by Christian educators are the traditional, pragmatic, social-science, or biblical approach.

The Traditional Approach

Continuing to provide ministries that served well in the past is important in the traditional approach, and energy is invested in revitalizing existing programs. In the search for workable ideas, traditionalists may ask: What did I enjoy as a child? What did my children respond to best when they were in Sunday school or the midweek children's club? Should we try those approaches again? Traditionalists may resist change because they fear losing the positive features of long-term programs. They value the tradition and faith that was handed down to them and may assume the means used in the past are essential for passing the faith on to the next generation.

The Pragmatic Approach

The driving question in the pragmatic approach is, what works? Pragmatists are always in search of what is working for others. When evaluating whether to pick up a new idea, several questions surface: Does the activity draw children in and hold their interest? Is the approach creative and fun? Could the people we have working with children in our church use the method, resource, or program? Pragmatists are aware that children's lives are filled with stimulating media, and they seek Christian education methods that are equally stimulating.

The Social-Science Approach

Some religious educators[1] believe the social sciences provide the most accurate description of the educational process. Since religious instruction is education, they consult the insights of social science to inform their ministries with children. In this view, the Bible and theology are important, but they are seen as the content in religious instruction not the sources for understanding the process. Social-science advocates point out the dangers of an overspiritualized view of religious instruction, which expects God to act outside of natural processes and which leads teachers not to worry about their preparation or effectiveness, because they trust God to do the teaching and the life changing.[2] Some who value the social sciences fear that when Christians begin with a study of biblical perspectives on education, the serious examination of findings from the social sciences is short-circuited.

The Biblical Approach

Many Christian educators believe strongly in the importance of Scripture as a source of guidance for all of life, including religious instruction and spiritual formation. They turn to the Bible in their search for insights on effective ministry with children. Some who give ultimate authority to Scripture question using the findings of social science, since much of the research is done by persons who do not embrace the Christian faith as they understand it. Although the findings of science may be helpful for knowing how to teach mathematics, it is assumed that secular research has little contribution to make in the understanding of Christian education or spiritual formation. Those who distrust the social sciences may claim to depend for guidance on the Bible only, not realizing that what one sees in Scripture or chooses to focus on is influenced by the experiences that have formed the person. As a result, the biblical guidelines they identify may sound like the tenets of the education that they experienced.

An Integrated Approach

Might it be possible that tradition, human experience, social-science research, and Scripture all provide insights for understanding a child's spiritual formation? Is there a way of bringing together the strengths of these approaches in an integrated search for truth and understanding? I believe there is.

Before discussing a method for an integrated approach, we need to examine the relationship between Scripture or theology and the social sciences—an issue debated by Christian educators. Ted Ward, an insightful Christian educator, presents an understanding of truth that makes possible an integration of theology and science. Ward begins with God as the source of all truth, which is revealed through God's

Figure 1 *Ward Model*

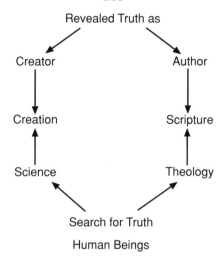

God

Revealed Truth as

Creator   Author

Creation   Scripture

Science   Theology

Search for Truth

Human Beings

Model developed by Ted Ward, then professor at Michigan State University (now retired professor of Trinity Evangelical Divinity School).

actions as creator and author (see fig. 1). The universe is the result of God's creative activity and Scripture came into being as the Spirit of God acted to inspire writers across the centuries. God created human beings with curiosity, a desire to know, and the ability to search for understanding and truth. The search for the truth about creation, we call *science,* and if human beings in relationship with one another are the piece of creation under study, it is *social science.* Theology results from our search for truth revealed through Scripture.

If God is the source of all truth, science and theology should be in harmony. When they are not, either our science has failed to capture the truth revealed in creation, or our theology has not adequately understood the revelation of Scripture and how it is to be applied. Apparent disharmony between science and theology should send serious Christians to look again at their understanding of both science and theology. While believing there is truth to be discovered, we must humbly realize that we do not possess absolute truth. We have our understanding of truth, which is colored by the influences that have formed us. As we grow in grace, experience more of life, study, and interact with other seekers after truth in various fields, we will discover the need to refine our understandings.

When evaluating the harmony between science and theology, it is important to differentiate between the findings of science and the application of those findings. In some cases social-science research may accurately describe the human being God created, but secular scientists, operating without biblical perspectives, sometimes draw conclusions from the findings that are inconsistent with Scripture. The Christian educator may take the same findings but in the light of biblical principles see different implications.

Leaders or ministers working with children in the church need a philosophy of education, an understanding of human development, and a theology that are in harmony, each area supporting the others. This calls us to be students of Scripture and the social sciences. If Scripture and science both offer insights on ministry with children, how can those insights be integrated into a rationale or theology of spiritual formation in childhood? Professor Melvin Dieter[3] describes the search for understanding in a model that enables one to build what he calls a dynamic molecule of truth (see fig. 2). It is a method for doing the theological reflection needed to guide ministry. Scripture is the core of Dieter's model, but Scripture is in dynamic interaction with tradition, reason, and experience. Let us look at how the parts of the model relate.

Figure 2 *Building a Dynamic Molecule of Truth*

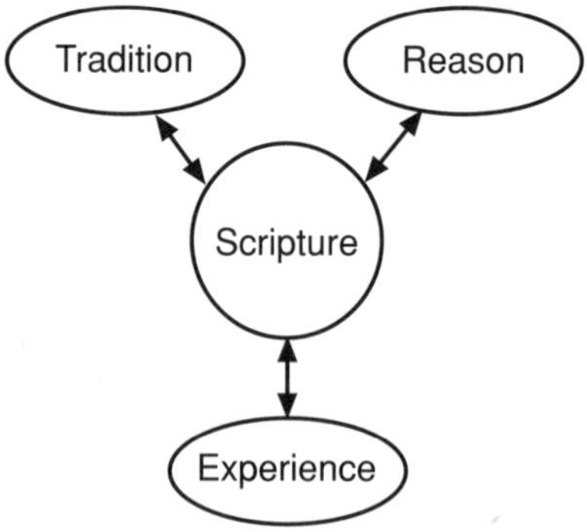

Diagram developed by Melvin Dieter, professor emeritus, Asbury Theological Seminary.

For Christians, Scripture—consisting of the Old and New Testaments—holds special authority as God's revelation to humanity. How Christians understand the nature of that revelation and authority varies greatly. My purpose is not to discuss different views on Scripture nor to defend a particular doctrine of revelation. It will be helpful, however, for you to know the assumptions about Scripture that guide my use of the Bible in formulating an understanding of the child's spiritual development.

Scripture provides us with our most complete revelation of God. That revelation comes through the story of God's interactions with the people of Israel, other nations in the Old Testament, and the church in the New Testament. In the life of Jesus we see God most clearly, as God became flesh and lived among us. Our main source for understanding God and God's ways is not a book of abstract statements about God but stories of God involved in the lives of individuals and nations and stories of God walking the earth in the person of Jesus. It gives us prayers and songs that flowed from the hearts of real people as they related to God in real life. It gives us sermons preached by prophets to people who had turned away from God, and letters to churches where new Christians were learning to live out their relationship with Christ together and in a non-Christian world.

The history and literature of the Bible carry the revelation of God and are the source of theology—our understanding of God and how God relates to the world. Through the inspiration of biblical writers, God chose this form of revelation. Stories, prayers, and songs flowing out of experience, and words of instruction to real people in specific contexts must be the best means through which God can be made known. Truth about God and what God values for human beings is found both in stories and commands or pronouncements.

To find God's truth, Scripture must be studied and interpreted.[4] Truth is not isolated—intact gold nuggets to be picked up from the pages of the Bible, strung, and worn as a theological necklace. Scripture as an authoritative source of truth about God and God's plan for persons must be interpreted with the aid of tradition, reason, and experience.

Tradition is sometimes defined as the way things were done in the past. The piece of tradition relevant to this book is what Christians in the past have done in their effort to encourage children in their faith. When looking at the past it is important to ask, what function was the activity expected to fulfill? The methods used may no longer be effective, but what those methods intended to accomplish may still be critical for faith development. Our challenge is to find methods appropriate to contemporary culture that provide our children with the enrichment children of earlier times found through the old methods. Too often people in the technological age think they are the first to learn how to do things correctly. As we look at tradition, we need a spirit of humility to discover the wisdom of the past.

Within the Christian faith, tradition also refers to the story of what God has done in the past among and through the people of God, both in biblical times and throughout church history. How have Christians in past centuries understood Scripture and God's will for the church? Their understandings are part of our tradition. Another aspect of our tradition are the rituals that symbolize the faith, give Christians identity, and connect them with the people of God down through history.

Tradition sheds light on the interpretation of Scripture when we see how Christians in other centuries and other places understood the Bible and applied it to life. But Scripture also provides a critical corrective for tradition. Some of our traditions hinder the building of God's kingdom—the work of the church—because they are based on misinterpretations of Scripture or are specific applications of important principles that, though appropriate for one point in history, are no longer effective. Scripture can also help us identify the basic functions that every faith community should provide for children. These functions become criteria for judging which traditions to carry on, modify, or abandon.

Reason is a human tool we use in our search for truth. Whenever we study Scripture, reason is active, interpreting and assigning meaning to what we read. Christian educators need to develop Bible-study skills for the task of sound interpretation. In Dieter's diagram (fig. 2), reason also represents knowledge discovered in many fields of study, such as education, psychology, or medicine. Reason can discover truth from the study of creation, which sheds light on the meaning of Scripture. It can also provide an understanding of how to apply biblical principles. For example, Jesus commands his followers to go and make disciples and to teach them to obey everything Jesus had commanded (Matt. 28:19–20). The Scripture gives the command but does not spell out the specific methods or means. Wisdom from the fields of education, psychology, and communication can amplify the meaning of Scripture and help us know how to fulfill the command.

However, Scripture also sheds light on other fields of knowledge by revealing error or incompleteness. For example, during the twentieth century, new discoveries in the social sciences caused people to believe that they had the understanding needed to solve the world's problems and to lead humanity into reconciliation and a perfect life together on our planet, but those hopes have been dashed by one outbreak after another of prejudice, selfishness, and hatred. In Scripture we learn about the fall and the devastating results of sin. This leads us to believe that any theory or understanding of human beings is incomplete if it does not recognize the fact of human sinfulness along with the belief in the greatness of human potential.

Experience teaches all of us and colors the way in which we perceive everything we study. There is no way to be totally objective about what we know. Our experience causes us to be fascinated by certain understandings or ideas and to hardly notice others. In the study of Scripture, some verses seem to leap off the page because of their relevance to our experience, and others we pass over without taking notice of them. Experience gives depth to understanding. For years we may believe and even teach a certain biblical command such as Paul's admonition to console or comfort others with the comfort with which God comforts us (2 Cor. 1:3–4). When we then suffer a great loss and God graciously comforts us, we come to understand the Scripture much more fully out of that experience.

Using experience in our search for truth about spiritual formation calls us to be attentive to the experiences of children and their parents. We must ask how children are experiencing life in their homes, communities, and the ministries of our church. Do responses seem to differ for the girls or the boys, the introverts or the extroverts, those whose parents attend the church or those whose parents do not, children with learning disabilities or the gifted? Are there certain settings or activities in which children seem to be most responsive to God or most likely to sense God's presence? What is life like for the parents of the children with whom we minister? We gain valuable insights as we observe experience.

Scripture comes into dialogue with experience in several ways. Much of Scripture is the story of life experience and God's involvement in and response to those events. From the Bible we get a glimpse of what children experienced in the Old Testament faith community and in a relationship with Jesus. Those pictures suggest components to include for children in the life of the faith community today. In the biblical stories we see ourselves and discover God's response to actions and attitudes similar to our own. Through the study of Scripture, light shines on our experiences, revealing need for change and confirming what God values. The commands and precepts of Scripture are to be learned not simply by intellectual exercise but through experience. As we try to live out those commands, Scripture has an impact on life—living the commands provides a fuller understanding of their meaning and importance.

As Christian educators, our search for truth must engage us in an ongoing conversation with Scripture, tradition, reason, and experience. Scripture evaluates the other sources and integrates them with biblical insights into a harmonious understanding. Tradition, reason, and experience help interpret and point toward the application of scriptural perspectives. New discovery in any of the four areas prompts a fresh exploration of the others.

The chapters that follow are designed to set the stage for such a conversation. Our search for insight into the spiritual formation of children begins with an exploration of Scripture. We then examine the findings of several developmentalists and persons who have investigated the spiritual potential of children. These findings will be woven into a comprehensive, integrated understanding of spiritual formation, which can guide those providing ministries with children and their families. You will be asked to reflect on your own experience and the practices of your church as it ministers with children. Hopefully, you will discover ways of enhancing those ministries.

THE FOCUS: SPIRITUAL FORMATION

Spiritual formation, spiritual development, spiritual growth, how faith forms—these are the phrases you encountered in the beginning paragraphs of this book. The focus of this study is not religious instruction, teaching, or Christian education but rather spiritual formation during childhood, which includes instruction but involves much more than the formal education programs of the church.

What is spiritual formation? The goal of spiritual formation is a maturing faith and a deepening relationship with Jesus Christ, through which we become more like Christ in the living of our everyday lives in the world.[5] The spiritual life is formed through practices that help to open the person to God and break down barriers that hinder his or her perception of God.[6] Spirituality involves the whole person relating to God and is not something laminated onto life.[7] True spirituality has an impact on every part of a person's being and is expressed through the personality in all relationships.

It is interesting to note that scholars writing in the field of spiritual formation tend to use the terminology of spiritual formation almost exclusively in reference to adults or older teenagers. The discussion of spiritual formation during childhood is seldom mentioned. But does spiritual formation begin in childhood, or is the maturity of at least adolescence needed before the spiritual life can be formed? From infancy the personality is forming; children are developing the elements of their personhood with which they will relate to God. They are becoming persons who will be inclined toward faith or persons who will find it hard to trust, persons who take the initiative, can stick with a task, and are ready to serve others or persons who do not believe they can make a difference in their own lives or the life of anyone else.

Author John J. Gleason Jr. believes that in the process of development there comes a right time for learning certain lessons at the unconscious, feeling levels. Because of this, persons are drawn to specific theological ideas at particular stages in human development; they will learn something about the concept at that time, and what they learn, whether accurate or distorted, profoundly influences their future religious learning. What they learn from these "subjective, gut-level experiences will carry more weight than" later, more superficial, objective, conscious lessons.[8]

The spiritual life of the child is forming at a deep level. Healthy personality development prepares children for openness to God, whereas developmental dysfunction creates barriers to a life of trusting, growing faith. To not be concerned about spiritual formation during childhood is to ignore the very foundations of the spiritual life.

Although psychosocial, cognitive, and moral development have an impact on spirituality, we must note that there is more to spiritual development. A biblical view presents God as the initiator of all spiritual life. The apostle Paul stated that we are saved by grace through faith and that grace and faith are gifts of God (Eph. 2:8). God graciously works in our lives, drawing us with unconditional love into a relationship, making possible our responses of repentance, faith, and obedience. God initiates but awaits our response, made possible through grace and faith.

Evangelical Christians believe conversion, the point at which one receives Jesus Christ as Savior, is critical to spiritual life. Conversion does not occur suddenly, out of the blue with no preparation. From the beginning of life God's grace is active on our behalf, forming us through experiences and relationships, making it possible for us to respond to God's love when the time is right.[9] Many children sense God's presence, love Jesus, and are captured by Bible stories. Those are evidences of grace. We will never minister with a child in whose life the grace of God is not active. Even the hurting, angry child can experience grace through our love.

W. W. Meissner believes grace provides an energy that "works in and through the ego," making possible spiritual dynamics such as faith and hope. If grace works through the developing ego, healthy development gives grace more to work with and enhances spiritual development. The negative resolution of developmental crises, on the other hand, hinders the working of grace, even though grace can have a healing effect on the ego.[10] Spiritual formation and ego development can and should go hand in hand.

Spiritual formation is a process for all of life, including childhood. In the following chapters we will seek to better understand how the spiritual life of the child forms and how we as adults in the faith community can enhance that formation. Some of what we discover will guide us in knowing how to effectively instruct children in the Christian faith, which can contribute to spiritual formation. But we also want to discover how to facilitate the healthy development of the whole person, preparing him or her to enter into a relationship with God. What helps children open up to God? What prevents or closes down an awareness of God? Finding answers to these questions will help equip us to be workers, together with God, for the spiritual formation of children.

two

CHILDREN IN THE BIBLE

How should we join with children on the spiritual journey? How do they come to understand and own their faith? Through the centuries, Christians have looked to Scripture as their major sourcebook. We, too, will start there in our search for insights.

When wondering about teaching the faith to children, many people focus on some form of school: Sunday school, vacation Bible school, Christian day school. If we hope to find the description of the ideal school for faith in the Scriptures, disappointment awaits us. Schools did exist in Bible times. During the exile (586–444 B.C.) the Jewish people developed synagogues. Since they could no longer worship at the temple in Jerusalem, they met at the synagogue to study the Law and to keep their faith alive. When they returned to their own land, they brought the synagogue home. After the temple was rebuilt, it became the place of worship, and the synagogue became the place of study. Adults studied the Law and children were taught the Law at the synagogue. Until the age of six children were taught at home; afterward they could go to the synagogue school to continue their education. In A.D. 64 attendance at the synagogue school became mandatory for Jewish boys.[1] Ezra or Nehemiah could have written about the synagogue school; the New Testament writers could have described the best procedures for teaching children in the synagogue schools, but the Bible is silent on the subject of instruction in schools.

The Bible is not silent, however, on how children are to be instructed and formed in the community of faith. The Book of Deuteronomy articulates the instructions Moses gave as Israel prepared to enter the Promised Land. Insights on teaching the faith to children are embedded in the bigger picture of God's plan for the people of God. We begin our search in Deuteronomy for a biblical perspective on the spiritual formation of children.

OLD TESTAMENT INSIGHTS ON NURTURING CHILDREN

Spiritual Formation in Everyday Life

Teaching was not an option for Moses—it was a direct charge from God. Moses was given the important task of teaching the people to observe, keep, and do the commands of God (Deut. 6:1–3, 6, 17–18, 24–25). The expected outcome was a way of life; learning was to be lived not just held as knowledge in the mind.

Fulfilling the charge to teach did not begin with teaching children. Moses addressed his teaching to all Israel—not to individuals or nuclear families but to the whole faith community (Deut. 6:3–4). The people of Israel needed to prepare for their teaching task with their children. After restating the Ten Commandments in Deuteronomy 5:6–21, Moses moves to a more basic level of instruction in chapter 6. "Hear, O Israel," he calls. "Listen, take this in":

> The LORD is our God, the LORD alone. You shall love the LORD your God with all your heart, and with all your soul, and with all your might. Keep these words that I am commanding you today in your heart. Recite them to your children.
>
> Deuteronomy 6:4–7

Note the points in Moses' teaching. He began by declaring Israel's vision of the one true God, who was their God. They believed in an active God who created, liberated, and revealed how to live. Everything rested on that belief in God. Secondly, Moses called the people not merely to a cognitive allegiance but to a love relationship with God. Thirdly, he stated that God's commands were to be internalized. The commandments were not to be an external restricting force but an inner commitment motivated by love for God, which would result in living God's way. James Fowler describes faith as a vision of the transcendent that impacts the total person and gives purpose and meaning to all of life.[2] Faith is the focus of Moses' teaching.

Only after adults had affirmed their faith in God, entered into a love relationship with God, and internalized God's laws were they really prepared to teach their children. The order of Moses' instructions suggests the importance of the teacher's faith in the effectiveness of instruction. Faith is the goal of teaching. Yes, there are stories and commands to be learned, but they are a means to an end. The goal is an awe-inspiring faith in God passed from generation to generation (Deut. 6:2); only persons of faith can pass on the faith. A concern for teaching the faith to our children must, therefore, involve nurturing the faith of the adults in the faith community.

Next, Moses commanded the people:

> Recite them [the commands of God] to your children and talk about them when you are at home and when you are away, when you lie down and when you rise. Bind them as a sign on your hand, fix them as an emblem on your forehead, and write them on the doorposts of your house and on your gates.
>
> Deuteronomy 6:7–9

The commands of God are taught best in the normal flow of life. Adults and children can talk together about God and God's ways at home, as you go here and there, at bedtime, and as you start the day. Whenever something causes you to think about God, talk naturally about God then. These would not be planned lessons but mini conversations about God as child and adult enjoy a flower, a song, or a story about God.

Parents can set the stage for natural conversations about God. Tapes of age-appropriate Christian music can fill the minds and hearts of children and adults with thoughts of God. These can play as families are at home or traveling. Parents can take time to enjoy nature with the children. Books about God's ways and Bible stories can become the child's favorites for nap or bedtime.

The people of Israel used visual symbols to remind them of God. When fathers prayed, they strapped to their left hand and forehead small leather boxes containing selected verses from the Law. Selected verses were also placed in little boxes called *mezuzahs* and attached to the doorposts of the house. Each time they passed through the doorway, the Jews touched the *mezuzah*[3] and were thus frequently reminded of God's Law.

What are the symbols in our homes? Do they remind us of God? By the door in my bedroom hangs a plaque that reads, "Jesus Never Fails." It is special to me not because it is great art but because it hung in my home during my childhood; it reminds me of my parents' faith, which became mine. When my nephew Paul was a baby, a picture of Jesus playing with a group of children hung at the end of his changing table so that many times a day he looked into the smiling eyes of Jesus. For several years a felt banner reading, "Paul, Servant of God," hung on his bedroom door. That concrete symbol gave Paul's parents a chance to tell him about the man for whom he was named. Today, Paul is a young man with a passion to introduce others to Jesus. Concrete symbols can provide opportunities for us to talk with our children about the things of God; the symbols, then, could remind them again and again of those conversations.

Deuteronomy 6:7–9 points to parents as primary teachers of the faith. They are the ones with children in the normal flow of life around home as they come and go, prepare for bed, and get up in the morning. God planned for parents to teach but not in isolation. Teaching in the family was to take place in the context of a whole community that lives the faith.

God's plan is for a community of families with shared values. The fact that the children's friends receive similar teaching and nurturing in their homes would enhance the parents' instruction. Other adults in the community would reinforce parental teaching. If tensions between parents and children blocked communication, other adults would be there for them. Parents also need the community to help them grow in their own knowledge of God and to support them in the process of being parents who can effectively nurture their children. God never intended two parents to bear the load of raising their children alone.

Later in the chapter, Moses stresses the importance of living God's commandments: "You must diligently keep the commandments of the LORD your God, and his decrees, and his statutes that he has commanded you. Do what is right and good in the sight of the LORD" (Deut. 6:17–18). God wants children to live in homes and a community where the laws of God are not just recited and talked about but lived. Children need to see and experience the faith in action. This experience would raise the child's curiosity. The questions would come: Why do we do this? What does it mean? Moses did not say, "If your children ask"; he said, "When your children ask . . ." (Deut. 6:20). The godly life will raise questions in the child's mind.

When the question comes, the child is ready to learn; it is a teachable moment. Much instruction blows past children because they are not ready for it. Their questions, however, give clues as to their readiness for learning. We cannot program questions into the minds of children, but when we have internalized God's laws and are motivated by love for God, we can live out our faith with integrity in the presence of our children, and the questions will come at the right time for each child.

Notice the kind of answer Moses instructs the people to give when the questions arise: "Then you shall say to your children, 'We were Pharaoh's slaves in Egypt, but the LORD brought us out of Egypt with a mighty hand'" (Deut. 6:21). In other words, we can tell them the story of God's work in our lives. Moses does not recommend a theological lecture; children benefit more by hearing the stories that carry the theology. For the Jews, the stories we find in the Old Testament were the stories of their families. Our children need to hear the Bible stories of the people of God, and they also need to hear contemporary stories of how God has worked in our personal lives, in our families, and in our faith community. Later we will come back to the role of story in spiritual nurture.

Before leaving Deuteronomy 6, notice one more point. Moses feared for the people of Israel.

When the LORD your God has brought you into the land that he swore to your ancestors, to Abraham, to Isaac, and to Jacob, to give you—a land with fine, large cities that you did not build, houses filled with all sorts of goods that you did not fill, hewn cisterns that you did not hew, vineyards and olive groves that you did not plant—and when you have eaten your fill, take care that you do not forget the LORD.

Deuteronomy 6:10–12

Moses was afraid they would forget God. Three times in Deuteronomy Moses voices this fear (4:9; 6:12; 11:16) and then, within a few verses, commands the people to teach their children (4:10; 6:7; 11:19). Teaching children is important for adults as well as children. As we tell children the stories of the faith, talk with them about God, and answer their questions, we refocus on God. Our love is rekindled as we remember God's acts, and as we wrestle with the questions raised by our children, we stretch and grow. We are on the faith journey together, and we need each other.

One outline of Deuteronomy titles chapter 6, "Covenant to be internalized and all-pervasive."[4] Before discussing specific religious practices, Deuteronomy presents the bigger picture or, we might say, the heart of the matter. God called the people of Israel not just to the observation of a few religious rituals but to a way of life that flowed from a heart of love for God and others. God's laws could become freely chosen habits of the heart. Internalized beliefs can impact all of life, making possible consistent integrity even when one is not thinking about those beliefs. That kind of living teaches powerfully.

Spiritual Formation through Ritual

As part of the way of life, however, God did prescribe religious rituals to keep the inner realities alive. These rituals were also a means of teaching the faith to the next generation. Deuteronomy 16 describes three feasts to be observed each year: the Passover (16:1–8), the Festival of Weeks (16:9–12), and the Festival of Booths (16:13–17).

As the people of Israel waited for the last plague to strike Egypt, they prepared for the first Passover (Exod. 12:1–28). Even then they knew they were to commemorate the event annually. Year after year, the Passover observances of sacrificing the lamb and eating unleavened bread with bitter herbs reenacted the first Passover and reminded the people of God's great deliverance. They celebrated their freedom from slavery, and the Passover observance created potent teachable moments. As the children experienced the event, they would ask, "What does this all mean?" and parents would tell the story of God's marvelous deliverance.

Over the years the Passover celebration changed. The whole sacrificial system, including the Passover sacrifice, ended when the temple was destroyed in A.D. 70. However, a Passover ritual based on the former observance developed, and that ritual actively involved the children. Now as then, the youngest person present at the Passover meal, usually a child, asks the questions that draw out the story. At the beginning of the meal a piece of unleavened bread is hidden; near the end, the children hunt for the bread, and the finder receives a prize.[5] There are activities and fun, as well as unusual tastes, a beautiful candlelit setting, stories, songs, and the reciting of Scripture, all experienced by the family together. Such a tangible, sensory experience powerfully communicates awe, wonder, and an identity with the people of God whose story is told.

The other two feasts, the Festival of Weeks and the Festival of Booths, were times of thanksgiving. The Festival of Weeks was a day of joyful thanksgiving to celebrate the completion of harvest. The Festival of Booths began with a celebration when everyone came together waving branches to praise God. For seven days families lived in shelters they had built from the boughs of trees. Children very much enjoyed these events. But why do it? They did it so that each generation would know their ancestors had lived in booths when God brought them out of Egypt—so that they would know the story and also know "I am the LORD your God" (Lev. 23:43).

During Bible times, each of these celebrations took place in the designated location for worship, which meant they were national celebrations. Families traveled to the tabernacle or the temple three times a year. Not just nuclear families but the people of God as a whole were bonded together as they worshiped their God and remembered his mighty acts for them. In those gatherings children developed a deep sense of identity.

The Hebrew word *yada* (know) carries the concept of involvement with that which is known.[6] This kind of knowing comes through experience. Jewish children knew their history as they experienced it in the feasts year after year. Through these repeated rituals, they grasped what they were ready to learn as they grew and developed.

Sensory Symbols of the Faith

The first commandment strictly forbids the making of any images to represent God (Exod. 20:4). There was no place for idols, but the religion of Israel was rich in sensory symbols. God gave specific instructions for the tabernacle, and later the temple, which would represent God's presence to the people. The tabernacle was no ordinary tent with its embroidered linen and fur coverings and its gold and bronze furnishings. Children would notice this and the care taken when it was moved.

The children with whom I worship are also fascinated with symbols of our faith. Children visiting our worship center are attracted to the colorful materials on the tabernacle story tray. Frequently they ask to hear that story, and I tell them how the people of God needed a way to come close to God. Children watch spellbound as I set out the ark of the covenant, the altar of incense, the table of shewbread, and the menorah. I then set in place the tabernacle with its outer room and the Holy of Holies. Next I move the priest figure into the tent, between the table of shewbread and the menorah, through the sweet smelling incense and smoke, through the veil into the Holy of Holies to be close to the ark of the covenant and close to God. One young worshiper, Mark, watched for the first time as I placed the coverings over the tent. "Oooh," he softly exclaimed as the fur covering was added. When the tabernacle was completed, David, another young observer, said, "I wish our church was like that," and Franklin, engrossed in the story, bent low to peek through the door.

Imagine children watching as the Levites took down the tabernacle or put it up again. There was mystery as the Levites carried the tabernacle furnishings. What precious things were under those blue or fine leather coverings?[7] There were beautiful textures and colors, the aroma of sacrifices, incense, and special meals—so much for the senses to take in as Jewish children participated in their religion.

Yet there was more. Earlier we noted the visual symbols of the Law, which parents wore. National monuments were erected as visual reminders. When the Israelites crossed the Jordan into the Promised

Land, they took twelve stones from the riverbed and set them up by their camp at Gilgal (Josh. 4:1–8). Joshua explained to the people:

> When your children ask in time to come, "What do those stones mean to you?" then you shall tell them that the waters of the Jordan were cut off in front of the ark of the covenant of the LORD. When it crossed over the Jordan, the waters of the Jordan were cut off. So these stones shall be to the Israelites a memorial forever.
>
> Joshua 4:6–7

Again God gave a means for stimulating the questions of children and the telling of the story.

After the first conquests in the Promised Land, Joshua called all the people together to renew their covenant with God. As Moses had instructed in Deuteronomy 27:1–8, Joshua built a large stone altar on Mount Ebal and offered burnt offerings to the Lord. While the people watched, Joshua wrote the law on the stones of the altar. Then he read the law, the promise of blessings, and the warning of curses. The children were there with their parents, and each time they saw the altar, they would remember that covenant renewal (Josh. 8:30–35).

Children and Adults Together

You will notice that the observances described above were for the whole community of faith. They were not events in which children participated while most adults were doing something else. Although some religious observances involved only priests or adults, many events included the children along with the adults. That was true on Mount Ebal; it was also true in a national crisis during King Jehoshaphat's reign (2 Chron. 20:1–28). As a great enemy army advanced toward Jerusalem, King Jehoshaphat was afraid. He called for a fast, and all the people gathered at the temple in Jerusalem to seek God's help. The children were there too, experiencing the event with their parents. They heard the king's prayer; he proclaimed God's greatness and power and recalled what God had done in the past. He declared their powerlessness in the face of the enemy and confessed, "We don't know what to do, but our eyes are on you, Lord." As the congregation waited, imagine the fear, anxiety, and desperate hope that charged the atmosphere. Then Jahaziel, a Levite in the crowd, spoke, "Listen, thus says the Lord. Do not be afraid. The battle is God's. Take your positions, stand still, and see God's victory." Early the next morning the army went out singing praises to God and discovered God had already defeated the enemy. As the king led the procession to the sound of trumpets and harps, all the people returned to the temple rejoicing.

What a way for children to learn about the God who acts! They were present to sense the human hopelessness and the need for God, to hear God's promise, and to experience the joy and celebration of the promise fulfilled.

Children were also part of the great celebration led by Nehemiah when the walls of Jerusalem were rebuilt (Neh. 12:27–43). Two choirs marched on top of the walls singing; harps played, and cymbals crashed. The choirs met at the temple, where they rejoiced and offered sacrifices. The children also rejoiced, we are told. Probably they had played in the rubble of the walls; some may have helped in the rebuilding. On the day of great celebration, one can picture boys and girls running along the wall, keeping up with the choir and orchestra, joyfully mixing with the crowd at the temple. Yes, the children were there as the people praised God.

Needed, a New Covenant

If these are such great means of teaching the faith, you may ask, why did Israel turn from God? A good question. Moses' fears for the people were realized. Their hearts were drawn away from God to the gods of those around them. When people no longer love God with their whole heart, religious observances with the greatest of potential become only hollow rituals, and the integrity of life and word is gone, draining events of their power to communicate the faith.

As Jeremiah preached to Israel prior to the fall of Jerusalem, God revealed what was needed if the people ever were to be what God desired them to be.

> The days are surely coming, says the LORD, when I will make a new covenant with the house of Israel and the house of Judah. It will not be like the covenant that I made with their ancestors when I took them by the hand to bring them out of the land of Egypt—a covenant that they

broke, though I was their husband, says the LORD. But this is the covenant that I will make with the house of Israel after those days, says the LORD: I will put my law within them, and I will write it on their hearts; and I will be their God, and they shall be my people. No longer shall they teach one another, or say to each other, "Know the LORD," for they shall all know me, from the least of them to the greatest, says the LORD; for I will forgive their iniquity, and remember their sin no more.

Jeremiah 31:31–34

We come back again to where Moses began with his teaching. Loving God with our whole being is required to consistently live the faith and teach it. History, however, shows how hard that is, but Jeremiah declared a word of hope. God will do something within a person, making it possible to truly know, love, and serve God.

NEW TESTAMENT INSIGHTS ON NURTURING CHILDREN

The New Testament is the story of the new covenant; a covenant that does not lower God's standards but points to the power to meet those standards. Because of the death and resurrection of Jesus and the coming of the Holy Spirit, a new power is available for living God's way. The church is called to be the people of God and to provide the nurturing community required to teach and to help people grow in the faith.

What does the New Testament say about teaching the faith to children? It is silent on specific programs and how-tos. The early Christians met in homes for worship, teaching, learning, and fellowship. Since whole families would be there, we assume children participated alongside the adults in the Christian community. The Scriptures of the New Testament church were the Old Testament, which provided them with the instructions we have already examined regarding children in the faith community.

Jesus' View of Children

It is in the life and teachings of Jesus that we find the most helpful New Testament insights concerning our ministry with children. The incarnation affirms the importance of childhood. When "the Word became flesh and lived among us" (John 1:14), God did not arrive as a mature adult. No, Jesus came as a baby and lived each phase of childhood. He knew the love and comfort of parents and the fears, sorrows, and joys of a child. He could be a friend to children.

Jesus valued children and took time for them. Parents wanted Jesus to bless their children. It was not enough for them to bring the boys and girls to see and hear Jesus from a distance, parents wanted Jesus to touch their children, to hold them in his arms, to look into their eyes, and to speak a blessing. Something about Jesus caused parents to assume he would bless their children. However, the disciples saw children as less important than adults; they did not want them bothering Jesus and taking his precious time and energy.

When Jesus discovered the disciples sending the children away, the Gospel of Mark records that Jesus was indignant. The disciples were depriving children of what was rightly theirs, and Jesus was angry. "Let the little children come to me," Jesus said. "Do not stop them; for it is to such as these that the kingdom of God belongs" (Mark 10:14). If the kingdom of God belongs to children, they deserve full welcome and participation; they need to grow up as noticed, valued, and nurtured members of the faith community.

Jesus took the time to hold the children in his arms, lay hands on them, and bless them (Mark 10:16). He gave the children personal moments with himself. Probably many did not understand the words of the blessing, but they could understand the love communicated through the touch and the smiling eyes of Jesus.

Jesus saw children as examples from whom adults should learn. When the disciples argued about which of them was the greatest, Jesus called a child to him and said, "Truly I tell you, unless you change and become like children, you will never enter the kingdom of heaven. Whoever becomes humble like this child is the greatest in the kingdom of heaven" (Matt. 18:3–4).

The size and power of adults impress young children. Realizing their own smallness and powerlessness, they know they need the protection and care of parents. Jesus says, be like a child in your relationship to God.

The word *children* appears 482 times in Scripture.[8] A large number of those occurrences do not refer to persons under the age of twelve but to persons in relationship with God. *Children* is a key metaphor picturing our relationship with God. Our study of children, their relationship to us as adults, and our responses and relationship with them can lead us to important new discoveries about God and our relationship with him. The longer I study children, worship with them, and examine what helps them know God, the more impressed I am that much of what is good for children is also essential for adults. Jesus invites us to approach the kingdom of God as children; only those who come in a childlike spirit will enter (Mark 10:15; Luke 18:17). We will return to this theme and its implications later.

As Jesus held the child and talked to the disciples about greatness and becoming like children, another concern was triggered in his heart and mind:

> If any of you put a stumbling block before one of these little ones who believe in me, it would be better for you if a great millstone were fastened around your neck and you were drowned in the depth of the sea. Woe to the world because of stumbling blocks! Occasions for stumbling are bound to come, but woe to the one by whom the stumbling block comes!
>
> Matthew 18:6–7

Jesus knew things would not go smoothly for children, but he declared that hindering children on their spiritual journey would be a serious offense.

How often do we hinder children or turn them away from the Lord just because we do not think about them and their place in the body of Christ? We do not often ask, "What do the children need?" or try to see things through their eyes. Without realizing what we are doing, we set children aside to wait until they are ready to come to Jesus as adults and to understand his teachings. We may even express our frustration at the clutter and noise of children's ministries or at the presence of children and, like the disciples, speak sternly to those trying to bring the children to Jesus (Mark 10:13). Those who study the spirituality of children discover the young child's heart is naturally open to God. How it must grieve the Savior to see little ones ignored or pushed aside when they are so ready to know and love Jesus.

Listen again to Jesus: "Whoever welcomes one such child in my name welcomes me" (Matt. 18:5). What is involved in welcoming? When we welcome someone into our home, we receive them with a positive attitude not just with tolerance. The focus is on the guests and enjoying them. We direct the conversation to include them and plan activities we think will appeal to them. When we see how they respond, we may even change our plans. Do our churches welcome children?

What does it mean to welcome a child in Jesus' name? We are called to welcome children on behalf of Jesus. Jesus wants children to experience his love in concrete ways through his disciples. As children receive consistent, unconditional love from us, we can begin to introduce them to Jesus and his love. There is mystery here. When we welcome the child in Jesus' name, we give the gift of welcome to Jesus. What a privilege.

Did you notice that Jesus speaks of children as "little ones who *believe in me*"? (Matt. 18:6, italics added). Some commentators claim Jesus shifts gears in verse 6 of Matthew 18 and begins speaking of humble Christians or young Christians when he uses the term *little ones*.[9] In verses 2–5 Jesus is pictured holding a child and talking about children; verse 6 then reads "*these* little ones." The flow of the text gives no reason to exclude children and replace them with humble or young Christians. Jesus named children as persons who believe in him; they have faith. They simply believe Jesus is real and trust his love. May we never cause them to stumble by looking down on their faith (Matt. 18:10).

Jesus healed children and at least once used an illustration from their dramatic play in a sermon (Matt. 11:16–17). Children were present at the feeding of the five thousand (Matt. 14:13–21), the feeding of the four thousand (Matt. 15:32–39), and likely much of the time when Jesus taught and healed publicly. Children were a welcome part of his life.

After the triumphal entry into Jerusalem, Jesus cleansed the temple and then healed those who came to him. The children were there still shouting, "Hosanna to the Son of David." When the priests objected, Jesus said, "Have you never read, 'Out of the mouths of infants and nursing babies you have prepared praise for yourself'?" (Matt. 21:15–16). Did the children understand the meaning of "Hosanna to the Son of David"? Probably not, but Jesus accepted the praise of their hearts as natural, valued praise to God.

MINISTRY WITH CHILDREN TODAY

The Vital Faith Community

What does all this mean for ministry with children today? From his study of Scripture, Lawrence Richards identifies five processes that he believes influence the growth of a child's faith:

1. communicating belonging to a vital faith community
2. participation in the life of a vital faith community
3. modeling of members of the faith community
4. biblical instruction as interpretation of life
5. encouraging growing experience of personal choice[10]

The setting for these processes is a vital faith community. Richards focuses on what we discovered in Deuteronomy: The vitality of the faith community is critical to the nurture of the child's faith.

John Westerhoff claims that religion, but not faith, can be taught. Faith must be inspired within a faith community.[11] Children's ministries cannot be done in isolation; it requires a community of faith. The spiritual health of the adults and the life in that community impact children. The faith of children is most likely to grow when they have the opportunity to associate with adults who are growing persons who know and love God. The child's faith is inspired when he or she belongs to an inclusive community that seeks to live out God's love. Look at your church. Is it a community where faith is alive? Those who care about children will work and pray for the spiritual health of the whole community.

Nurturing Parents

The nurture of parents is of special concern for children. As Moses began with instructions to adults, we too must provide for the equipping of parents. Many adults feel inadequate for the challenges of parenting and may be drawn to a church that offers help. Often church classes give parents formulas and long lists of dos and don'ts. We imply that anyone can follow the plan and become a perfect parent with all problems solved.

Robert D. Hess offers valuable insight on parent education. He believes parents learn how to be parents not in a classroom but through interactions with their children. Relating to their children in each child's present phase of development is an all-consuming task. For this reason, parents are more apt to pick up on tips that apply to present parent-child relationships. They do not tend to stockpile insights and ideas from class sessions on parenting for future use. Hess found that many parent education programs that intended to encourage good parenting were actually discouraging to parents. In the classes parents heard that they

> probably do not have the competence needed for child-rearing; second, knowledge and techniques for dealing with children are available; third, if they wish, they can acquire these skills. A fourth message is implicit but unavoidable—if parents are not successful, it is their own fault.[12]

When their competence is questioned, parents lose confidence in themselves. When they try a new technique that does not work or they fail to use the skill taught last week, discouragement and guilt set in.

According to Hess, parent support groups are better than a parenting class approach to parent education. A support approach acknowledges the complexity of child raising. If parents know that their task is difficult, they are not devastated by a failure; if they think the job is easy, their confidence is undermined when they fail. Feeling inadequate, they avoid further information that they assume will make them feel guiltier and less competent.

In support groups parents discuss the experiences they have with their children and how they deal with different situations. Learning that others face similar problems and feel negative emotions and frustration with their children gives parents great relief. This release allows them to hear and learn from one another. Experience as a parent gives authority and credibility to the suggestions shared by group members.[13] Together, week by week, they grow in their effectiveness as parents.

Probably the most important element in parenting is the parent-child relationship not competency in certain skills. Richards suggests that in our equipping we should focus more on the parent and less on methodology.[14] The church can encourage parents to participate in a group in which they are nurtured spiritually and supported as they learn what it means to live out the laws God is writing on their hearts. Living out God's love and grace in relationship with children would be part of what these groups could explore. This can be a setting for seeking out adequate answers to the difficult questions children ask; such a search may be a means of parents coming to know God more fully.

As groups of parents explore God's Word together and share their lives, they can support one another as they build values into their families. Their children, then, will have friends whose families share their values and reinforce parental teaching.

For several years I belonged to a Bible study/prayer group made up of couples with young children, older couples whose children were grown, and singles. All of us lived a great distance from our parents, brothers, sisters, grandchildren, nieces, and nephews. We became an extended family for one another. Earlier we noted that God never intended parents to raise their children in isolation. The church has the potential to be a wonderful extended family in our mobile society, but too often the North American spirit of independence leaves us sitting lonely and overburdened in our pews with unrealized support and care all around us. We are convinced that if we are worth our salt, we can do it alone, but that is not God's way. God created us for relationship—to need each other. God wants the church to be the family of God, to be there for one another, supporting, caring, and growing together. For most people, however, this will happen only if leadership in the church finds ways of helping people connect.

Families benefit from tips on how parents can set the stage for talking about God in the normal flow of life. Do your Christian education leaders provide parents with the songs and verses their children are learning at church? What about having a parents' meeting once a quarter when parents can sing the children's songs and discover what they will be learning? This could happen during a special Sunday school class, a Sunday potluck, a mothers' morning out program, or a men's breakfast. If the songs being used are on tape, encourage parents to buy the tape. Stock the church library with books, videos, and tapes for children and parents. Include ideas for family activities in the church newsletter. Advent, Lent, and Easter are good times for special family activities. In the newsletter or in a Sunday school class, suggest ways adults can get to know and express greater interest in the children of the congregation, how older couples could adopt a family, or how younger families could adopt grandparents, an aunt, or an uncle.

With our hectic lives, how many parents and other adults will join a group? How many will use the suggestions offered? At first very few may respond, but start with the few and let the involvement spread as word gets out on the benefits experienced.

Including Children

In our study of Scripture, we saw that children were included in the events of the faith community. Richards highlights the importance of communicating a sense of belonging to children and allowing them to participate in the community.[15] These two processes are intertwined; the sense of belonging grows as one participates.

Over the last few decades, the number of separate age-level activities has increased in many churches. Age-level activities are important; children, teenagers, and adults need to develop peer friendships. Various age groups are interested in particular content areas and are helped by exploring concepts at age-appropriate levels. However, healthy spiritual growth also calls for participation in the life and events of the faith community as a whole.

Some churches include children in intergenerational worship each Sunday, while others seldom have children worship with adults. Still others have children worship with adults and teens for the first part of the service before going to children's worship. Whatever a church decides on children's worship, children need to be part of some congregational worship experiences throughout the year.

I am not speaking of deciding to include the children for certain events with no consideration of their presence. If children are expected to be present, the service should be planned with them in mind. Welcome children specifically. Mention them and their concerns in prayers; invite them to participate in various parts of the service, such as prayer time at the open altar. The congregation might sing a chorus or a hymn the children have learned. The pastor could include one or two sermon illustrations from childhood, since everyone present has been a child and can relate. Children, and many adults, benefit from changes in position and sermons and readings that are not too lengthy. Sensory experiences such as banners, candles, or palm branches to wave engage the attention of children. Remember, Jesus asks us to welcome the children. Therefore, as we plan intergenerational events, we must plan for the children as well as the teenagers and adults.

As a child growing up, the highlight of the church year for me was the Christmas program when children, youth, and adults all had a part. Many opportunities for meaningful participation can be offered to children throughout the year. Children's choirs can minister to the whole congregation regularly. Older children can read Scripture or serve along with adults as ushers. Young children can help an adult straighten hymnals and pick up papers after a service. Children can do very well if adults take the time to help them learn how to perform the tasks. In the process of helping children prepare to minister and in doing ministry together, important relationships can develop between child and adult. When we know one another and are known, identity builds. Working together with adults, children have the opportunity to follow the example of those adults.

You are probably thinking this sounds like a lot of work. True, it is easier to do it ourselves and not to worry about the children outside the programs designed for them. But remember, Jesus valued children profoundly. Jesus says, let the children come to me. Do not stop them with boredom or by simply entertaining them in another location until their parents finish worshiping. Welcome them in Jesus' name. Make adjustments that will serve them, knowing that adults benefit from what helps children learn. And do not look down on their faith; it is real, beautifully simple, and alive. Never forget, it is as important to nurture the faith of a child as it is the faith of a teenager or an adult.

Three

FOUNDATIONS FOR FAITH

I held three-week-old Katie, studying her little nose, perfectly formed lips, and tiny fingers and feeling the warmth of her body in my arms. How beautiful. What potential was wrapped in that tiny person? Who would she become? Beside me sat her mother. Kris and I had prayed for Katie before she was conceived; we celebrated and prayed for her again when we knew she was on the way. From the couch across the room, her seminary-student father enjoyed watching me meet his little daughter. We talked of ordination and of the church where he would serve after graduation. Big brother John played among us and with three-year-old expertise gained our attention, gently caressed Katie's head, and kissed her. Proud grandparents looked on. How will this family impact who Katie becomes? How will the church family into which Katie moves influence her?

All those who care about Katie want to be contributors in her development. But what makes our influence most positive? An understanding of how children develop will help us know better how to relate to them and what to provide for them. The work of Erik Erikson offers significant insights into the development of children and the role others play in that development.

ERIKSON'S THEORY OF PSYCHOSOCIAL DEVELOPMENT

Erikson invested much of his life in the study of children. His experience with children began as a teacher and continued as a child psychoanalyst, trained by Anna Freud. For years he worked with children using play therapy to help them express what was going on inside them. With anthropologists, Erikson studied the child-rearing practices of American Indian tribes and analyzed the impact of those practices on the kinds of persons their children became.[1]

As a psychoanalyst, Erikson talks about the id, ego, and superego. Sigmund Freud identified these as three parts of the human personality. The id is the irrational, impulsive, and selfish part of the person, which seeks pleasure and wants that pleasure immediately. The ego is the rational side of a person, which begins to develop as an infant becomes able to use cognitive functions such as perception, learning, and problem solving. The ego organizes experiences and tries to make meaning out of them. It also tries to serve the id by finding acceptable ways of dealing with the id's demands, or it may block the demands of the id and in this way master it. The superego is what we often call conscience. Children take in as their own the moral values and standards of their parents; the superego is like the voice of the parent in the child's mind reminding him or her of what is right or wrong, making him or her feel guilty or ashamed after violating a rule.[2]

Although Erikson's perspectives are rooted in psychoanalysis, his emphasis differs from that of Freud. He placed more emphasis on the impact of social influences and less on sexual urges as the driving force of development. In Erikson's description of development, the rational ego is more central than the irrational id. He also describes the potential for development across the life span, rather than looking only at childhood and warning of the lasting impact of childhood traumas.[3]

Erikson saw human development as the process of the body and the ego developing in interaction with the social context.[4] None of these elements can be fully understood in isolation from the others, and all must be considered to comprehend human development. It is the interplay of biology, psychology, and the social that causes development and accounts for its outcome.

Erikson held a holistic view of persons, believing that biological and psychological development could not be separated. He noted that as the body uses physical abilities, such as sucking, and gains control of body functions, the ego develops psychological abilities comparable to the physical ones. Bodily pleasure impacts the developing ego, and psychological anxiety always causes tension in the body, which may result in pain and illness. The physical and psychological are intertwined.

Individuals cannot be fully understood without looking at the social setting in which they develop. Relationships with family, friends, and community powerfully influence our development throughout life. The degree of success persons experience in living up to social expectations affects their view of themselves. Anxieties in the family or community show up in the anxieties of individuals. The developing body and ego are susceptible to the tensions and concerns in the social environment.

Erikson believed we are influenced by the history of our family and community as well as by present dynamics. Experiences of the past affected our parents and their parents before them; those experiences reach across time through who our parents became, and now they touch us. The stories of who we have been as a family, a community, or a nation affect our expectations, perceptions, and responses. When those stories are recounted and celebrated, their influence increases. Erikson's theory of human development takes into consideration the complex interplay of physical and psychological development interacting with other persons and their history. He labeled the development he described *psychosocial*, believing that the person and the social could not be split.

Stages of Development

From his extensive study of human beings, Erikson identified eight stages of psychosocial development (see table 1).

Table 1
The Psychosocial Stages of Erikson

Stage	Age Range
1. trust versus mistrust	birth to 1 year
2. autonomy versus shame and doubt	1 to 3 years
3. initiative versus guilt	3 to 6 years
4. industry versus inferiority	6 to 12 years
5. identity versus role confusion	12 to 20 years
6. intimacy versus isolation	20 to 40 years
7. generativity versus stagnation	40 to 65 years
8. integrity versus despair	65 years and older

Erik H. Erikson, *Childhood and Society* (New York: Norton, 1985), 247–73. Specific age designations from Carol K. Sigelman and David R. Shaffer, *Life-Span Human Development*, 2d ed. (Pacific Grove, Calif.: Brooks/Cole, 1995), 269.

What does Erikson mean by *stage?* Before exploring the characteristics of stages one through four, we will examine some of the dynamics involved in the stage concept of development. Erikson did not view persons as static things moved from one stage box to another. When he spoke of the human organism, he had in mind a "process rather than a thing."[5] Healthy persons are never static; they are always in process, responding and becoming. They cannot be explained by a stage label, but an understanding of the dynamic processes in which they are involved at each stage can give insight into the person.

A stage, then, is a phase of life when the person is dealing with certain challenges, developing new capabilities and a new sense of the self in relationship with others. Because of these changes, the person perceives and experiences life in ways qualitatively different from what goes on in other stages. Movement from one stage to the next is caused by a configuration of changes occurring about the same time in the life of the person; the body changes, emotional and cognitive growth occurs, and society expresses new expectations. As the child or adult responds to these changes and manages them, development takes place.[6] The challenges of one stage are resolved, and the person moves on to the challenges of the next.

Developmental laws within the human organism cause physical development to occur in a predictable sequence. Within a certain age range, we expect babies to be able to hold their heads up, sit, stand, and then walk. We know generally when to expect teething, the onset of puberty, or menopause. There is a normal pattern in physical development, even though the precise timing varies from person to person. Biological development sets the stage for psychological development, causing children of similar ages to deal with common psychological challenges. A given society tends to have age-related expectations for their young. The biological and social patterns, then, combine to place each psychosocial crisis in a predictable period of life.[7] These factors also cause psychological crises to arrive whether or not the individual is prepared to handle them. Even if persons have not successfully completed one stage, the challenges of the next move in on them.[8]

In describing developmental stages, Erikson identified conflicts and crises. He believed crises come, in most cases, from a normal set of stresses rather than from a great trauma. Society places demands on the child such as expecting five-year-olds to leave the safety of home and go off to the new world of kindergarten. Stressful psychological effort is needed to resolve the crisis created by the child being away from his or her mother and by having to learn to get along with teachers. By describing crises in each stage, Erikson implied that normal development does not proceed smoothly and painlessly. Crisis is to be expected. Stress will be experienced at each stage because the skills one brings from the last stage are not adequate for the demands of the new stage. Growth, with its pains, is needed to meet the new expectations.[9]

The labels Erikson used present the crisis of each stage in terms of the positive and negative possibilities for resolution. From a mix of positive and negative experiences, each person resolves the crisis of a given stage somewhere along the continuum, from the very positive to the extremely negative. For example, one baby may develop a deep sense of trust, another may be basically trusting but reserved with strangers or in new situations, while yet another may distrust everyone. Those who care for children want to provide experiences that contribute to developing positive qualities. Shielding children from all negative experiences, however, or despairing when we fail at some point is not healthy. Negative experiences can be instructive and contribute to growth.[10] For safety's sake, we must question the trustworthiness of others and know how to assess a relationship before giving ourselves to it. A degree of self-doubt allows us to use autonomy wisely. For healthy development the person must process and integrate both negative and positive experiences.

Although many people resolve crises on the positive side, each succeeding stage becomes more complex and challenging, with the result that negative resolution is more likely. The positive resolution of one stage provides ego strength and new skills to take on the demands of the next, but a negative resolution at one stage makes it very difficult for the person to resolve future crises positively. Having to move into a new stage without completing the work of the previous one leaves the person handicapped for dealing with new crises.

The satisfactory resolution of a crisis does not mean the issue is mastered for life. Erikson realized that many hazards threaten the healthy view of self and others achieved at a given stage. New inner conflicts or changing external circumstances can threaten our capacity for trust, autonomy, initiative, industry, or identity.[11] We will need to deal with these crises and to help others address them across their life span. Now, with this process in mind, we turn to an examination of the developmental challenges that face children.

Trust versus Mistrust

Before birth the healthy baby's needs are continuously met. Held close in the womb, the child experiences absolute security. Then comes birth; the infant is forcefully pushed into the big, cold world. The baby faces a crisis; arms and legs stretch out frantically, helplessly, and for the first time there is nothing there. Comfort comes when the little body is again enfolded, this time in a blanket and in the arms of a parent. But the agenda has been set; the baby has a crisis to resolve, a question to answer. Can the new world be trusted to respond and meet the baby's needs? Is it a safe place?

How infants resolve the crisis of trust versus mistrust depends greatly on the baby's caregivers. Babies cry to let the world know they have needs; they reach out for comfort. When someone comes to hold, feed, and change them, they learn that those around them can be trusted to respond. Instant response on every occasion is not necessary to teach trust, but if the mother and other caregivers come consistently, before the baby's frustration gets out of hand, the baby will remember this pattern of dependable care, and the foundation for trust will be laid.

Feeding, changing, and holding give comfort. As infants spend more time awake, they enjoy repeated sensory games and interactions with those close to them. These feelings of comfort and enjoyment are associated with the people who care for and interact with the baby. Mother, father, siblings, and others become part of the good feelings the baby experiences.

For most children the first strong relationship is with their mother. The amount of trust babies develop depends on the quality of the relationship with their mother, not just on whether she provides food and dry diapers and demonstrates love. Erikson found that babies developed the greatest trust when mothers combine "sensitive care of the baby's needs and a firm sense of personal trustworthiness within the trusted framework of their culture's life."[12] The mother who has learned to trust and feels affirmed by a supportive community communicates that trust to her baby in intangible but real ways. Who we are flows through to the babies we care for.

Erikson believed the parents' sense of meaning is communicated to their children. For the parents, is there a purpose, a reason for living? Do they have a place in a larger community that helps them develop values and goals that integrate and make sense out of the pieces of life? Meaningfulness gives parents a confidence that babies can sense; this builds trust. When parents see the loving nurture of their baby as a major part of their life purpose, the baby is included in their sense of meaning, and the baby feels cherished.

Parents need to have an idea of the kind of person they are becoming and they want their child to become. The community or society to which they belong can give the parents a vision of that good person.[13] How parents care for their children and why they respond as they do is an important influence on the kind of persons their children will become. Parents may respond to the baby's cry unpredictably based on their own level of tolerance at the moment, or response may be guided by the kind of person the parents hope the child will become.

Response guided by a vision of the kind of person the child could become was demonstrated by Lloyd as he closed the door, leaving his daughter Christi crying in the bedroom. "I've fed and burped her, changed her diaper, rocked her, and I'm sure nothing is wrong. If she insists on making that noise, she can do it by herself where the rest of us don't have to listen." Lloyd believed it was important for Christi to become a person who respected the feelings of others. If she needed to vent her frustration she could, but not in a way that made the whole family miserable. The value of respect for others guided Lloyd's actions, not his momentary frustration.

Learning to fit into the ways of a family and a culture is often frustrating for children. Erikson found, however, that children can endure that frustration best when parents have a reason for the restraints they impose, and that reason is valued by the society to which they belong. The restraint then has meaning.[14]

The faith of parents, Erikson believed, provides important support for the child's emerging sense of trust.[15] Faith and a trusting relationship with God give parents a sense of confidence and meaning that communicate peace and trusting confidence to the baby. Erikson also noted, however, that some parental religions are detrimental to the building of trust. Distorted views of God as a demanding judge or a father whom it is impossible to please may cause parents to be fearful and insecure themselves or harsh and demanding with their children.

Another quality that is essential to relationships and builds trust is mutuality—a give and take between infant and adult. Often adults operate as if they are solely in charge of relationships, the ones who change and shape the child, but the arrival of that tiny infant changes the parents' lives forever. Babies are not passive lumps of clay; they are active in relationships, modifying and regulating the parents and others who care for them. Babies reject or end interactions by fussing, crying, or going to sleep. They call us to them with their cries and reinforce interaction by smiling, cooing, snuggling, and maintaining eye contact.[16] Both baby and adult learn; the parent learns what different cries mean, what the baby enjoys or finds comforting, the normal patterns of sleep and play. As the parent comes to know the baby better, it becomes easier to meet the child's needs. The baby learns what gets the desired parental response and that the comforting response can be expected.

Enjoyment can also be mutual. The feeding infant spends many hours in comfort, gazing into the mother's or father's eyes. Those eyes can mirror love and deep value for the child. Adults communicate pleasure as they try to get an infant to smile or talk back to the baby's cooing. In these mutually enjoyable encounters, the baby feels cherished and the inner sense that "I'm all right" takes root and grows. These mutual relationships in the early months of life can set the pattern for relating to others in the future.[17]

Healthy relationships must be mutual. Babies are not served best by excessively responsive parents. If babies always get what they want when they want it, they can take control. This may not be good for the baby's health or the health of the parents. Babies who always get their way through incessant fussing fail to learn more positive ways of interacting with others. They are not learning what others like and dislike or how to behave in ways considerate of those around them. Babies need tender loving care, but parents who give no thought to their own needs may be starting their child on a life of extreme self-centeredness.

Babies first approach things to take them in, learning to get what they need.[18] Through sucking and swallowing they take in food. Soon babies are able to take in with their eyes—studying faces, gazing intently at a mobile over the crib, or following the movement of a person working near them. They also take in through their skin, which increases in sensitivity and in the hunger for touch.[19] As babies are held and caressed, they take in love, comfort, and security.

The baby learns how to get mother's attention with a hungry cry. When feeding is a time of warm relaxation, a time of receiving nourishment and feeling the comfort of being held, when the mother's eyes reflect enjoyment and love, the baby begins to believe in "friendly others" who can be trusted to give. Erikson believed learning to get from a "friendly other" is important in learning to be a giver also.[20]

With a growing sense of trust, babies can face their greatest fear—separation from mother. Their first social achievement is to be able to let mother out of sight without suffering overwhelming anxiety. This can be done only when the memory of mother's consistent care and frequent returns makes the baby certain she will come back.[21]

Erikson believed that establishing a sense of trust leads to the basic strength of hope.[22] Hope, rooted in trust, gives optimism and the energy to seek new ways of coping with difficulty and challenge.

The ability to trust is fundamental to health, wholeness, faith, and maturity in all of life. We never outlive the need for trust. If in infancy or later in life a person develops mistrust, wholeness and maturity cannot come until someone or some community gives the opportunity to experience love, acceptance, and care that can be trusted.

The ability to trust is inseparably bound up with faith. Faith is reaching out to God in confidence that God will be there and will work for our good. If I do not believe the significant people in my world can be trusted to respond to my needs, why would I believe an unseen God would respond? Iris Cully says, "Children will develop a basic trust in themselves, others, and God through living with adults who trust themselves, other people, and God."[23] As children sense the cherishing and love that go beyond the perfunctory meeting of physical needs, they can also experience the calmness and confidence of a person with trusting faith.

Autonomy versus Shame and Doubt

During the second year of life, muscles mature rapidly, children master the skill of walking and physically become ready to control sphincter muscles. They begin using words and show an increase in their ability to coordinate various functions such as bodily sensations, actions, and words. These developments prepare two-year-olds to take on the challenge of establishing their autonomy. In stage one, separation from the mother was the baby's greatest fear, but as children begin to move around and explore, they enjoy this new freedom and discover that separate is good—autonomy is desirable.

As sphincter muscles mature, toddlers are able to experiment with holding on and letting go. Erikson saw this physical reality as an analogy of psychosocial activities important during this period of life. The physical activity of retention or elimination compares with the psychosocial activity of holding on or letting go.[24] Being able to decide when to hold on and when to let go is an expression of and an exercise in autonomy, both in the physical and the psychosocial realms.

The changes in the toddler that take place at about two years of age are a shock to parents, even when they have heard about the "terrible twos." Learning to stand, walk, say the first words, and build an interesting, expanding vocabulary are fun for the child and the parents. Together they celebrate each success. But then the battle to assert autonomy and control suddenly breaks out; two-year-olds discover the wonderful word *no*. To affirm they have a will of their own, they declare no even when they mean yes. They hang onto resistance with their stubborn no's. "Mine!" they shout and cling to a toy. On the other hand, they can lovingly share a treat with another child, choosing to let go of what is theirs. This is a period of great ambivalence; one minute the child snuggles lovingly then suddenly pushes the adult away, wanting to stand alone.

In establishing independence, children insist, "Me do it." They persist at trying, letting the adult help only when they know they can go no further themselves. The tenacity of their efforts is to be admired. "Doing it myself," however, calls for great patience on the part of adults, who could do it so much faster and easier. But when parents patiently support children in their efforts, the children increase in competence.[25]

As parents prepare to guide toddlers in toilet training and in controlling their outbreaks of self-assertion, it is important to remember again that a child is not a lump of clay to be forced into a rigid mold of expectations. Children need to develop the self-control of appropriate holding on and letting go by participating in the exercise of control. They need the privilege of gradually choosing to exercise their will to control bowels and other behaviors that need to come into line with what is socially acceptable. Parents need to work with the child's readiness for control and to be willing to let the learning extend over the time necessary, which will vary from child to child. If control is demanded before the child is able to deliver, he or she is deprived of the choice to control and instead fails. Children who are not allowed to freely choose to meet the demands will feel powerless and doubt their ability to choose self-control.[26] Such experiences lead to shame and doubt. Persons who doubt their ability to control themselves may eventually turn on themselves with the overcontrol of a severe conscience inflicting the letter of the law to control their behavior.[27]

A healthy environment for toddlers provides room for physical movement and choice combined with affirmation and reassuring control. Children need to assert and exercise their autonomy and control, but as they do so, they are vulnerable. Can the world be trusted to respond affirmingly even when the child demands to "do it myself" and holds onto what is "mine," even when the efforts result in spilled milk? Adults offer toddlers a great gift when they give age-appropriate choices, accept the spilled milk as a necessary part of learning, and affirm the choice to try as well as celebrate successes. Care must be taken not to shame children when they fail to control the bowels or bladder. When antisocial behavior must be restricted, the focus should be on the unacceptable behavior, not on an unacceptable child. When two-year-old Tiffany bites the baby while pretending to kiss him, her mother could respond, "No, Tiffany, Mother cannot let you hurt the baby." But she should not say, "Why are you so mean?" Protecting the child's sense of self-esteem is important.

In this stormy period of life, children must be protected from themselves by firm outer controls. They have not yet learned when it is appropriate to hold on or to let go, what they are capable of doing and what is beyond them. Shame results from a sense of being exposed.[28] If the choices and efforts of toddlers are not guided, their limitations and inabilities are exposed, and they experience shame and self-doubt. Unbridled antisocial behavior may incur shame-creating responses from adults and other children.

If children are not taught how to do new things, they may be defeated, which can lead to doubts about themselves and even shame.[29] Children who receive no guidance in their activities also face the danger of unfocused frenzy. They rush from toy to toy without focusing long enough to explore and enjoy any activity. Such patterns of frenzy can inhibit the possibility of taking initiative at the next stage.

Young children need limits that provide a sense of security and guidance. But those limits must give enough space for free and healthy expressions of autonomy. It is important for children to experience both firmness and tolerance, because this sets the stage for them to understand law and grace.[30]

Children who gain self-control without losing self-esteem develop the ego strength of will. If adults overcontrol them, children never develop self-control and become vulnerable to shame and doubt. Erikson found that the use of shaming to control children does not lead to genuine acceptance of the desired behavior. Instead, shaming stimulates the secret determination to try and get away with things unseen and to do what is needed to save face in the future. Shaming may even result in defiant shamelessness.[31]

We cannot protect children from all shame, but we can teach, guide, and affirm them so that they have the ego strength of will with which to face shame and doubt. Erikson defined *will* as "the unbroken determination to exercise free choice as well as self-restraint, in spite of the unavoidable experience of shame and doubt in infancy."[32] The strength of will that equips a person to take on the challenges of life and to keep going in the hard times is born in the experiences of the toddler. The way in which adults guide children as they establish their sense of autonomy has long-term impact and importance.

Notice that Erikson defined will as a combination of free choice and self-restraint. Children soon learn that experiencing the goodwill of others depends on individuals limiting the expression of their wills. Erikson believed children are assisted in the task of accepting self-restraint when the adult world around them is guided by principles of law and order. When those principles guide adult expressions of autonomy, parents and others have a sense of dignity and independence, tempered by an ordered consideration for the dignity and independence of others. As children experience this managed autonomy of the important adults in their lives, they have confidence that they, too, will be able to manage their autonomy.[33] The social setting gives meaning to self-restraint and strengthens the child's will to coordinate free choice and restraint.

Initiative versus Guilt

Erikson noted that around the age of four children seem to suddenly "grow together," both in person and in body. They have mastered the coordination of their arms and legs so that they walk and run without thinking about it. Their mobility and self-control have opened to them a much wider world. To their autonomy they now add initiative. Initiative involves understanding, planning, and attacking a task. It is self-designed and purposeful activity.[34]

In developing a sense of autonomy, children discover what they can do and establish a strong sense of who they are as individuals. In the initiative stage they turn to explore the outer world. Their newly acquired self-control gives them the confidence to experiment with the world around them. They take action, observe the consequences, and discover how things work and what brings desired or unpleasant responses from other people.[35]

Erikson observed that four- to six-year-olds seem to possess a surplus of energy. They are able to forget failures quickly and move on with zest to try the next experiment with its risks.[36] Eagerness to learn

and to make things characterizes them. They are ready to work cooperatively with other children and are open to learn from important
adults, such as teachers. They enjoy taking on obligations, which indicates they are bigger now and can do what adults do.[37] Aggressively
they move out into the world to make their presence known; physically they attack things with energy, enjoy competition, want goals,
and find pleasure in conquest. They intrude into the minds of parents
and friends with incessant talk and questions. Consuming curiosity
leads them to explore the unknown.

During this period of life, conscience begins to form. The conscience of young children is predominately the voice of the parents
speaking in the mind and memory of the child. Children accept as
their own and internalize the standards of right and wrong that their
parents communicate to them. Even when parents are not present,
children hear the inner voice, which causes them to observe their
actions and guides them toward right responses.[38]

Children internalize the voices of both father and mother, so if the
standards of the father and mother are contradictory, this creates a
problem for the child. Which voice should be obeyed? The child will
suffer guilt whichever voice is obeyed, because the other voice has
been disobeyed. Children need not only the moral words of parents
but also the example of ethical living in the family. The moral integrity
of parents is important, because children build into their conscience
the standards they see lived out in the home.[39] If children accept standards from their parents that make it impossible for them to engage
in certain behaviors without feeling guilty and then discover a parent
trying to get away with that behavior, a deep hatred of that parent
may fester. If parents do not live guided by conscience, children lose
faith in the reality of goodness and come to believe that arbitrary
power controls all.[40]

Guilt is the inner voice of conscience saying, "That was wrong. You
should not have done it." Guilt can be a healthy safeguard and corrective that triggers remorse and a desire to make things right. As
empathy grows, children become aware of times when their actions
hurt another, and their guilt can lead them to repair the damage done.
Knowing the negative feeling of guilt helps children resist the temptation to violate the inner warning voice of conscience.

A severe conscience, however, can make a child feel excessive guilt because of a simple accident or for situations over which the child has no control. Children often blame themselves for the divorce of their parents, the death of a sibling, or their mother's depression.[41] Wishes and thoughts a child could never act on sometimes create far greater guilt than deeds actually committed.[42] Children may blame themselves for the death of a parent or sibling simply because of a feeling of anger or a wish to be rid of the person. The child's sense of guilt is overwhelming, and if it is not recognized and addressed by a knowledgeable friend or counselor, that guilt can fester within, causing problems throughout life.

Parents can help avoid inappropriate guilt by being careful to differentiate between the behavior and the child when reprimanding their children. Parents must communicate that although the behavior is unacceptable, the child is accepted and loved. If children come to see themselves as fundamentally bad, they feel guilty for who they are. Guilt becomes crushing, and they feel there is no use trying to initiate anything good.

The conscience, then, can guide and protect the young child, or it can create inhibiting bondage. A healthy conscience guides without crushing and is firm yet flexible enough to handle the complexities of our changing lives.[43] Such a conscience forms when children live with clear, consistent guidance and boundaries so that they know what is expected but are given room to make choices, take initiative, and express individuality. If rules from parents and caregivers are uncertain and inconsistent, children have no clear voice to take in to guide them when faced with moral choices. If children are given rigid rules for every detail of life, there is no room for freedom or initiative— they are forever breaking the rules and feeling guilty.

Identification is the process through which the crisis of initiative versus guilt is resolved. The desire to identify with the same-sex parent is strong, and children love doing things together with the parent as equals. In this companionship the child's guilt over unacceptable feelings of jealousy or anger toward the parent is resolved, and the child also learns how to be a man or a woman.[44]

Play is significant to this psychosocial development during early childhood when children are fascinated with adult activities and roles. As they play house, school, restaurant, or firefighter, they are experimenting with being men and women. Erikson believed that play is to children what thinking, planning, and blueprints are to adults.[45] In play children explore roles, relationships, and consequences; they can try out and compare different options. From admired parents children picture an ideal self-image. In the process of identification they try to incorporate characteristics of their parents into their own behavior. As their behavior conforms to the ideal self-image and moral guidelines given by their parents, self-esteem is enhanced, and they experience self-confidence, which empowers initiative.[46]

The virtue or strength established through the positive resolution of the initiative versus guilt crisis is purpose. "Purpose is the courage to envisage and pursue valued goals uninhibited by the defeat of infantile fantasies, by guilt and by the foiling fear of punishment."[47] Purpose gives a sense of direction. It can be energized by creative imagination and fantasy, but one must know the difference between what is possible only in fairy tales and what could happen in real life. Young children are developing that differentiation. Knowing what is possible and a healthy conscience that knows what is permissible will set limits on purpose without inhibiting the pursuit of the purpose. Children are then released to invest their initiative and sense of purpose to pursue adult tasks. That pursuit begins with learning the basic skills such as reading and writing, which are needed for adulthood.

Industry versus Inferiority

In most societies it is around the age of six that adults begin to teach children the skills necessary for adult life. Education is the process by which children tackle the crisis of industry versus inferiority. Through education, adults pass on to the young the wisdom and skills of earlier generations. In the past this was done informally as children and adults entered into the life of the community, working alongside parents at home, interacting with neighbors, and participating in the family's religious life.[48]

As societies became more complex, many children no longer saw their parents at work. They did not have the privilege of participating with parents in the workplace where they learned to master skills and pick up attitudes. They could no longer learn what they needed for adulthood through informal means, so schools were established to teach children. Now the school is a culture of its own, which establishes goals for itself. The school may connect with family and community values, or it may establish its own goals, standards of achievement, and causes of disappointment.[49] School is a central influence in the life of the six- to twelve-year-old; it represents the larger society to children and thus becomes the voice of that society. Whether children expect to find a place in society may be based on whether they succeed or fail at school.[50] What happens there impacts them profoundly.

Erikson believed children of school age "like to be mildly, but firmly coerced into the adventure of finding out that one can learn to accomplish things which one would never have thought of by oneself, things which owe their attractiveness to the very fact that they are not the product of play and fantasy but the product of reality, practicality and logic; things which thus provide a token sense of participation in the real world of adults." Psychologically, school-age children are ready to develop a sense of industry, to move on from being engrossed in play and imagination to doing real work.[51] Children learn to win recognition by producing projects, demonstrating knowledge, or performing skills and are dissatisfied with nonproductive activities. The imagination is harnessed as children begin to learn to read, write, solve math problems, and work cooperatively.

A sense of industry develops as children use what they learn and eagerly participate in completing projects. This sense of industry exists when the productive activity is satisfying enough to hold children to the task, when the satisfaction of doing an activity is stronger than the desire to go play. The goal of teachers and parents during the elementary school years is to teach children the pleasure of work that is completed through perseverance. Industry also has an important social component; it involves doing things with others. Children need to learn the skills of cooperative endeavor, and in doing so they begin to discover how a society works together productively to provide for the good of all.[52]

Obviously, children do not suddenly become industrious and lose all interest in play on their sixth birthday. They develop a sense of industry through gradually experiencing the pleasure of a job well done. Good teachers know how to give children a balance of play and work. They also take into consideration individual differences. Some children are ready for more work and less play sooner than others.

Some learning tasks are difficult for certain children, while others are a pleasure. Effective teachers can encourage children through recognizing special effort invested in a hard task and can give them opportunities to enjoy using their special gifts.[53]

For some children who do not receive affirmation and encouragement, the elementary school years are difficult. Instead of developing a sense of industry, a deep sense of inferiority may settle in. Many factors contribute to feelings of inferiority. Physical and mental limitations can hinder children in mastering required skills, causing them to judge themselves inferior. Societies place high value on some abilities and devalue others; two prime values in America are reading and sports. The child who does not excel in these areas finds it very difficult to compensate and feel successful. The child's limitation may simply be rooted in a normal maturation rate that is slightly slower than other children. But by the time children with the slower developmental timetables are ready to learn to read, for example, they may already have decided that they are stupid and cannot do it. They may choose to avoid the expected failure by not trying to learn.

The way people in a child's environment respond to failure can stimulate feelings of inferiority. One message often given is, "If you had really tried, you could have succeeded," which questions the child's motivation. Other messages imply the child is not capable of success at the task. Children who receive messages such as these soon develop a sense of helplessness. They conclude that since they apparently do not have the right motivation or abilities, they are hopeless. These children believe they do not have the ability to change the outcome, so they make no attempt to learn from their mistakes or find out how they can do things differently to avoid failure in the future.

Children face judgment from within as well as from without. They are prone to compare themselves with their peers and to be devastated by the differences they discover. Unfortunately, some school-age children are shamed for their failures. It does not take many such experiences to cause children to avoid trying anything new for fear of shameful failure. Children who develop doubts about themselves in earlier stages and carry a sense of guilt will be prone to feelings of inferiority.[54]

Sadly, loss of self-esteem may also be caused by circumstances over which the child has no control. Adults at school and at church tend to be more responsive to the well-dressed, clean, attractive children, giving them special attention while ignoring others. Children may be teased mercilessly by peers because of some physical characteristic such as large ears or because they speak with an accent or a lisp. Some children cannot afford to participate in many special activities at church and feel excluded. When racial prejudice exists, children are viewed through the lens of a stereotype that expects them to fail.

Over time, children who are ignored or teased come to believe they are not worthy of special attention, that they are seriously flawed. When they cannot perform as well as others, or adults around them do not believe they can succeed, these children begin to feel inferior. Their self-esteem and confidence are undermined, and as a result, they may never reach their full potential. The whole society suffers when, because of low self-esteem, a person's gifts are never fully developed and used.

Those working with children should regularly ask themselves, "Am I overlooking any of the children while giving too much attention to others?" Middle-class Americans are often out of touch with the financial stresses in many families. When planning outings and events, make sure it is possible for all children to participate, either by selecting affordable activities or by providing scholarships.

We as adults are responsible for making our classrooms and club programs safe places for all children. When you begin working with a new group of children, let them know that you want everyone to be safe. Inform the children that you will not allow anyone to cut them down or ridicule them, and that the same is expected of them. We can do much to create a safe, nurturing environment if we take the initiative.

Usually we are blind to our own prejudices, but the Holy Spirit can open our eyes to them if we sincerely pray for that insight. And the power of God's love can overcome prejudice as we choose to love and welcome all God's children. As we, guided by the Holy Spirit, begin to discover each child's gifts, we can affirm these gifts and help the children build their self-esteem.

Learning to get recognition for what one can do is part of the process leading to the development of a sense of industry. Affirmation for doing well is an important motivator for children, but it also holds a danger. Children may come to believe that they are what they can do and that they must earn love, acceptance, and worth through performance.[55] Parents and other adults give children a precious gift when they affirm them for who they are, not just for what they do.

Children who successfully navigate the crisis of industry versus inferiority develop the ego strength of competence. Competence is the freedom to use skills and intelligence in completing serious tasks uninhibited by a sense of inferiority. It leads persons to willingly participate with others in productive work, confident that they can learn and serve the community.[56] A sense of competence provides strength to face the challenges of adolescence into which children then move.

EXPLORING IMPLICATIONS

Erikson believed the effectiveness of leaders in his day was limited by a major blind spot in their thinking. As they sought solutions to the problems of society, they ignored childhood. They made no connection between the ways in which children were raised and how they functioned as adults. No importance was attributed to the formative processes in childhood when considering causes or solutions for social ills.[57]

Church leaders suffer from a similar blindness. Although we claim to value children and give lip service to the importance of their Christian education, reference to their spiritual formation seldom becomes a significant theme in major strategies for the church. Often senior pastors leave the care of children to support staff and volunteers without having integrated the nurturing of children into the big picture.

Many pastors and teachers seek to understand adult spiritual formation in isolation from childhood spiritual formation. But our life stories are all of one piece; the experiences and responses of childhood are the foundation stones of personality and faith. Many adult problems in relationships with oneself, others, and God are the result of faulty development in childhood. The adult problems defy solution unless the childhood experiences and their importance are understood and addressed.

The church needs a new awareness of the importance of childhood. Children are now becoming the persons they will be and are laying the foundations on which to build life and faith. They are being formed through what they experience in their homes, schools, and the faith community. We must not be satisfied with giving them one or two lessons a week in formal Christian education settings. Our concern for the formation of children must embrace the family and the school as well as the church. What can the church do to help parents provide the family experiences needed for positive resolution in each stage of childhood development? What do children need to experience in the life of the church? Let us look at Erikson's insights on child development and see what they suggest for the church's ministry with children.

Beginning Spiritual Formation

Did you notice the words Erikson used to talk about the strengths in human development: *trust, hope, will,* and *purpose?* These words have a theological ring; they represent the concerns of Christian education. Human development and spiritual formation are not two separate, unconnected processes. True, spiritual development is more than biological, psychological, and social development, but healthy psychosocial development is an important part of spiritual formation. It sets the stage for a relationship with God.

The ways in which parents care for their baby, guide the toddler, and encourage the school-age child are all part of spiritual formation. God's design is to work through the everyday relationships of parents and children to provide children with experiences that prepare them for faith. David Seamands calls this parental grace.[58] The mother who with consistent, patient love cares for her infant gives that child his or her first experiences of trustable, unconditional love—grace. As she gives the baby reason to trust her, the way is prepared for the child to trust God. When parents give toddlers room to express their autonomy and are patient with their efforts to do new things yet set wise limits, they are preparing their children to understand God's laws and the freedom of will God gives each person. From the ways in which parents and other adults respond to their efforts, successes, and failures, children build their assumptions of how God will respond to them. Foundations for faith are being laid through the everyday interactions of children and adults.

Many parents feel inadequate to nurture their children spiritually; their own faith may be new, their biblical and theological knowledge limited. But God does not call them to be theological instructors; God calls them to parent lovingly and responsibly and to be on the faith journey themselves. When this is so, they will give children the grace gifts essential to their spiritual formation. Understanding Erikson's insights on healthy development can help parents relate to their children in ways that will lay a good faith foundation.

Parental Formation

Erikson discovered that the faith of parents, or their lack of it, impacts children. The parents' ability to trust and their sense of meaning influence the child's sense of trust, meaning, and worth. Erikson also believed healthy development requires that the parents and family belong to a larger society or community that helps them establish values and affirms them as they order life in accordance with those values. People who care about the spiritual formation of children must be concerned about the spiritual formation of the parents and their finding of a place in the faith community.

Who are the young adults who will be establishing their families in the next decade? You may hear them called Baby Busters, Thirteenth Generation, Generation X, Xers, or the Twentysomethings. They are the children of the Baby Boomers, born between 1961 and 1981. A hard look at this generation is sobering: Over half of them have divorced parents; one in three has suffered physical or sexual abuse; most of their mothers worked, and they became the first latchkey kids. They grew up surrounded by corrupt leadership: Watergate, the Contra Affair, moral failure of television evangelists and police officers. They have grown up with violence on the streets, at school, and on television. Although all generations of young people have had their problems, dysfunction and trauma are the norm for Generation X.

William Mahedy and Janet Bernardi, in their book *A Generation Alone*,[59] claim *aloneness* most accurately describes Generation X. Many were abandoned by fathers after divorce and received only limited attention from working mothers. They had to raise themselves and came to feel they could trust no one. Not having received the basic affection all children deserve, they did not connect with their elders and society. They feel alienated, like strangers in their own land. With technological advances and more educated people than there are jobs,

Xers feel unneeded. All this—and more—adds up to a generation that does not trust, that suffers from lack of self-esteem, and for whom life seems meaningless. Given the importance Erikson placed on the parents' sense of meaning and ability to trust, we can see how difficult it would be for these young adults to be the parents their children need.

If we look again at Generation X, however, we see signs of hope. Many of these young adults realistically acknowledge the bankruptcy of our self-centered, materialistic society. They are spiritually hungry, desire a sense of meaning, long for trusting relationships, and want to give their children the stable family they did not have. Those young adults who are not abandoning themselves to hopeless meaninglessness are turning to community as their hope. Even though trust is difficult, they know that they must have relationships and that they can find answers only in community. Left alone, Generation X cannot give their children what they need; however, many young adults are longing for a community of genuine, loving people with whom they can learn to trust and find meaning.

The church must step into the void and provide the community that Generation X seeks. In small groups, young adults can learn to trust. Their emptiness can be filled with friends, and, even more importantly, they can meet God and experience the filling of the God-shaped space within. Together they can study Scripture and discover moral guidance and an understanding of God's plan for living. As they begin to serve others in and through the faith community, they will experience the joy of being needed. Healing and continual growth can be experienced in these small-group communities.

The church is also able to provide community across the generations. Erikson noted with interest the definition for *trust* in Webster's dictionary: "the assured reliance on another's integrity." In Erikson's theory, trust is the ego value in the first stage and integrity the ego value of the last.[60] Trust builds as we are in relationship with persons of integrity. When the church lives as the family of God, friendship with mature Christians whose lives demonstrate integrity is a gift the church can offer the young.

Since young parents are deeply concerned about being good parents, parenting will be a frequent topic of discussion and area for support in their small groups and classes. The insights from Erikson included in this chapter could be shared in the small-group setting with discussion questions to assist young parents in exploring how to implement the ideas in their homes.

The spiritual formation of children should begin with the spiritual formation of their parents. As a church we must understand young adults, invite them into the community, and provide for their ongoing growth. Given the brokenness of our society, this is absolutely crucial. Incorporating young adults into the faith community must be a top priority for the church. The importance of the faith community to the family should be communicated by pastors in marriage counseling and when discussing the baptism or dedication of an infant. Since many Xers desire to be good parents, a "Preparing for Parenthood" seminar could be a port of entry for some young couples. Coming for parenting know-how, they might find community and stay to meet Christ and mature in faith.

Children in the Church

Erikson also provides guidelines for those who minister to children in the church setting. An annual retreat or workshop session for the children's ministries staff could be used to introduce teachers to Erikson's perspective on development and to discuss the implications of insights gained. Knowing this theory would help teachers understand the significance of their relationship with children and point them to ways in which they could enhance the development of the children in their classes. They would also become aware of the challenges children face during each stage and the importance of the developmental work they are doing. The following paragraphs highlight a few implications from the theory and suggest, in broad strokes, possible applications for various age levels.

The church nursery must be a trustable place. Are there familiar faces to greet the babies from week to week? In churches with a rotating staff in the nursery, it is best to have at least one person who is there consistently. Are there enough nursery workers to meet the babies' needs promptly and to hold those crying for comfort? In the nursery few spoken lessons are taught, but babies can experience church as a trustable, comforting place. They can be enfolded in the trusting faith and love of those who care for them. That is significant.

From Erikson we learn the importance of balance when relating to children. Toddlers working to establish their autonomy need room to express their independence both physically and psychologically, but they also must have external controls to protect them. They require firmness with tolerance, freedom to choose, and appropriate restraints. Four- and five-year-olds also depend on consistent guidelines and the expression of clear behavioral boundaries with which to develop their conscience, along with opportunities to take initiative and to make choices. The affirmation given school-age children must balance commendation for what they do with appreciation for and acceptance of who they are. Keeping these elements in balance calls for a teacher who has the ability to be flexible and responsive to children and who has the wisdom to know how much of each contrasting component to provide. It is crucial that teachers understand the importance of both kinds of responses.

Teachers must also be persons of integrity. It is important for children to see that those who teach moral standards also live them. The old adage reminds us, "What you are speaks so loudly I can't hear what you say." When the teacher's life does not come up to the standards he or she teaches, seeds of disgust are sown. Such teachers may contribute to children turning their backs on the Christian faith and rejecting Christian moral values when they grow up.

As children begin to develop new skills such as reading, writing, singing, or playing an instrument, they can feel affirmed in their worth if they can make real contributions at church. It is important to find ways for all children to contribute with their various levels of maturity and different gifts. Sunday school teachers face the challenge of allowing children to demonstrate their reading and writing abilities, while at the same time not embarrassing children whose skills are not as developed. Choirs are an excellent way for many children to minister to the whole congregation, and nonsingers could read Scripture in a worship service or play during an offertory. Take inventory: How does your church encourage children to take a meaningful part in the work of the church? Which children have not found a place? What might interest them? With whom might the child work?

Encourage elementary Sunday school classes and midweek groups to take on service projects in the church and community. They could clean up after a service, pick up litter from the church property, visit shut-ins, or make banners or displays for special congregational events. One group of children in a class studying the meaning of the Lord's Supper made the communion bread, which the pastor shared with the whole congregation. Instead of only classes working together, teachers might encourage families to take on service projects. When designing a ministry survey for use in your church, be sure to include tasks that children could do and encourage them to make a ministry commitment. Be sure to express appreciation for what children do; this recognized service builds their confidence and gives them a sense of belonging within the faith community.

These are only a few possible responses to Erikson's theory. Look again at his description of development. In your church, what might teachers do to help children positively resolve the crisis of each stage? What else could you do to equip parents so that their parenting more effectively assists their children as they lay their foundations for faith and life? Let the insights of Erikson give guidance as you evaluate and plan your ministry with children.

Four

YOUNG LEARNERS
IN ACTION

Kara sat beside me merrily sharing bits of five-year-old wisdom as we drove through rural Ontario. "Oh, look at the cattle," she suddenly exclaimed. "I believe they call those perverts." I responded with a gentle, "Might they be Herefords?" With excitement she went on, "Maybe, but you know there are lots of kinds of cattle. The black and white ones are holsteins, those are the perverts, and I don't know what you call the others." I had not realized how many Ontario farmers were raising Hereford cattle until Kara identified each herd of "perverts" as we passed them in the fields.

After Kara was safely in bed that evening, I told the story to her parents. We laughed together and then they asked each other, "Where did that come from?" When Kara's even-tempered father was disgusted with someone, I learned, he would sometimes say, "What a pervert." We decided *Hereford* had probably sounded like *pervert* to Kara, and she must have concluded that she finally had the meaning for the undefined word that had puzzled her. Children's efforts to figure out things have generated many funny stories and also have prompted some adults to try to understand how they think.

Early in the 1920s as Jean Piaget, a young Swiss psychologist, conducted intelligence testing, he became fascinated by the thinking of children. Their answers to the IQ test questions intrigued him—particularly the incorrect ones. How did children come up with those answers? This interest launched Piaget on a study of children and their cognitive development that lasted more than fifty years.[1] His research consisted of intensive observations of children in the normal flow of life and of interviews that attempted to reveal the processes of the children's thinking and to discover what caused those thinking processes to change.

Adults tend to assume that children are most like them in their thinking and least like them in their feelings. Piaget discovered that the reverse is true. We believe that all children need is more information and they will understand things our way. On the other hand, we often demand that children obediently stop in the middle of a fascinating project or television program and come to supper, without a thought for how they feel about being interrupted—without comparing their feelings to ours. Piaget found that children are most like us in feelings; they, too, experience frustration over interruptions. They are least like adults in thinking; more information does not make them think like us until they develop certain thinking processes. Children are intellectual aliens in the adult world; adult thinking is foreign to them.[2]

To communicate effectively with children we must learn how they think. The research of Piaget provides helpful insights into the working and the development of the child's mind. This understanding is important for adults who desire to facilitate the spiritual formation of children. Why? Because children think about God, reflect on Bible stories, and understand behavioral standards with the same thinking abilities they use in other areas of life. In this chapter we will examine Piaget's understanding of cognitive development.

ACTIVE LEARNERS

Piaget found that human beings are active learners from birth. The mind is not like a mirror passively reflecting whatever is held up to it;

rather, the mind is like an artist creating its own interpretation of what it sees.[3] Babies arrive with the inherited tendency and ability to explore the world around them and to try to make sense of it. They take in what they see, hear, and experience, organizing their perceptions of those sights, sounds, and circumstances to make meaning from them. Thinking is made up, then, of two components: content (sights, sounds, events, information, commands) and structure (the way in which the content is organized and processed).

Piaget used three words to describe the process of mental organization: *assimilation, accommodation,* and *equilibration.* To assimilate new information, we simply take it into an existing mental category or structure. Accommodation calls for the changing of a category or the establishing of a new one so that there is a place where the new piece of information or experience fits.

Eighteen-month-old Todd watched little brown creatures fly to and from the feeder by Grandpa's patio. "Those are birds," Grandpa informed him. "Can you say 'bird'?" Todd has formed a mental category for birds. "Bird," he shouted with confidence as a bright red cardinal, a large dove, and a blue jay came to the feeder. Each bird was assimilated into his category for birds, and his knowledge about birds expanded as he discovered they come in different colors and sizes and they chirp, sing, and sometimes fight for a place at the feeder. Then Todd saw a butterfly. Since it flies, he assumed it must be a bird and assimilated the butterfly into his best existing category. "No," corrected Grandpa, "that's a butterfly." Todd must accommodate then by adding a new mental category into which he can assimilate the butterfly.

Many times children—and adults also—assimilate information into a category where it does not fit. Kara's story at the beginning of this chapter is an example of this. She had a category for the word *pervert* but had no meaning in it. Probably because the words sounded similar, she erroneously assimilated "Hereford, red and white cattle" into the *pervert* category. In assimilation, input is modified to fit inner categories, whereas through accommodation, inner thought structures are adjusted to fit more closely with new discoveries.[4]

When a person or an experience suggests that our understanding—our way of categorizing certain things—is not accurate, that causes what Piaget called disequilibration. Our competence is questioned, causing a sense of inadequacy and inner discomfort. That triggers the desire to restore equilibrium—to set in motion the process of equilibration. Our inner sense of adequacy is restored when we accommodate our thinking, adjusting the categories to more closely reflect reality.

Going back to Kara, she was so confident in her new knowledge about cattle that my question, "Might they be Herefords?" did not create disequilibrium. Because of her joy in the new information she had assimilated, she was not ready to hear the question that pointed to the need for accommodation. Both assimilation and accommodation are important, lifelong processes. Understanding expands as we assimilate, and development results from accommodation as thought categories change. Accommodation does not occur on the demand of parents or teachers; it requires readiness. Later in this chapter, we will discuss the causes that influence readiness for accommodation and development.

Since children, teenagers, and adults are always organizing and processing the information they take in, understanding is constructed by the learner, not transmitted from one person to another. Some forms of instruction seem to assume that the concept of the parent or the teacher can be fully captured in words and then transplanted, through the ears of the hearers, into their minds. This view of instruction sets the stage for failure. As adults, we can give children content—information and experiences—as material with which they can build understandings, but each child must construct his or her own concepts. They blend what we give them with other bits of information they have picked up and organize it all, using whatever thinking processes they have developed. Their constructions are their own and may or may not be similar to the concept we intended to communicate.

When I was three or four years old, I announced to my parents that I did not want to go to heaven. Some of my elderly friends from church had become ill and died. My parents told me that they had gone to heaven, assuming that would comfort me. As the pastor's daughter, I had visited my friends during their illnesses and may have been with the families after the deaths. Being around sick or crying adults made me very uncomfortable. Out of all these experiences I was constructing my concept of heaven—a place full of sick and crying adults—and I wanted no part of it.

There is no way to keep children from building incomplete or incorrect understandings. However, we can take children seriously, listening for troubling misunderstandings and providing the missing piece of information or the experience that may bring comfort. We can learn how their thinking processes work at different ages, and then we will know how to assist them better as they construct the understandings most appropriate for their level of development.

THE PATTERN OF COGNITIVE DEVELOPMENT

From his study of children, Piaget identified four stages or periods of cognitive development. In each of the stages the child's thinking and logic are qualitatively different. Piaget labeled the stages:

sensorimotor or practical intelligence—birth to age 1 1/2 or 2
preoperational or intuitive intelligence—age 1 1/2 or 2 to 7 or 8
concrete operations or concrete intellectual operations—age 7 or 8 to 11 or 12
formal operations or abstract intellectual operations—beginning at age 11 or 12[5]

Piaget believed that all persons go through these stages in the same order, although the rate of development varies from person to person. Two factors keep the sequence of stages invariant. First, biological development, which follows a common sequence for all persons, prepares the way for cognitive development. A certain level of maturation must be reached in the brain before specific cognitive mental activities can be performed. Second, at each stage skills are developed that are necessary for moving into the next stage. The work of one stage provides the foundation on which the next stage is built.[6] A look at the characteristics in each of the stages will clarify how they build one on the other and what the difference in quality of thinking is at each stage.

Sensorimotor or Practical Intelligence Stage

From birth until the beginning of language development, the infant's mind works with sensations and actions, taking them in and organizing them. We might say, babies' actions are their thoughts. At first their actions are reflexes. In response to hunger, the baby cries, and someone comes to feed him or her. The baby's fist accidentally touches his or her mouth; the baby begins to suck and discovers it is soothing. When the results of a reflexive or chance action are satisfying, the actions are repeated and become habits. As babies grow and begin to play, they notice when something interesting results from an action, and they repeat the action trying to cause the result again. They begin to connect their actions with the results, discovering a simple form of cause and effect.

Babies next begin to experiment with new means for obtaining desired ends, at first through experimental actions and finally by forming the action plan internally.[7] Although they do not have words with which to think, the intellectual processes of infants are active and developing. Piaget states:

> There is no basic difference between verbal logic and the logic inherent in the coordination of actions, but the logic of actions is more profound and more primitive. It develops more rapidly and surmounts the difficulties it encounters more quickly, but they are the same difficulties of decentration as those which will appear later in the field of language.[8]

According to Piaget, babies learn things in a sensorimotor way that they will not master in verbal expression for years.

Egocentrism

Newborns are totally egocentric; they are completely unaware of anything other than their own body and actions. They make no differentiation between themselves and other objects; everything is an extension of themselves. They are unable to decenter from the self, to use Piaget's term. As time goes on in the first eighteen months of life, babies discover that they are an object in a world of objects.[9] This is the first act of decentering—the first step on a lifelong journey away from egocentrism toward an ever expanding ability to take the perspective of others.

Object Permanence

Another important learning in the early months of life is that when people or objects are out of sight, they do not cease to be. At first, when babies drop a toy, they do not search for it because for them what they no longer see does not exist. Once they learn that objects have permanence, it is not so frightening to them for mother or father to leave them. The game of peekaboo gives great pleasure to babies as they master the reality that those who disappear have not ceased to be; they will return.

In this sensorimotor period, children learn to walk and begin to use words to identify objects and to express desires. As language develops, they move into the next stage.

Preoperational or Intuitive Intelligence Stage

Between the ages of one and one-half or two and seven or eight, children amaze us with how much they learn. They master language in far less time than it takes an adult to learn a second language, gain a basic understanding of life in the family and in the communities in which their families participate, and begin the formal learning of school. The world of preschoolers and early elementary children is full of new things to be learned. They constantly take in—assimilate— their perceptions of events and the comments they hear, adding the new information into existing mental categories. Whether or not they have organized the data correctly and have made the right meaning out of it are not questions they ask.

Egocentrism

Human beings, even into adulthood, tend to believe themselves until others confront them with conflicting evidence. Adults usually assume that they are right even though experience has taught them that they ought to question and check out their assumptions. Young children, using what Piaget calls *intuitive intelligence,* do not question their thinking, because they are unaware that other people may have a different view of things. They are egocentric in perspective and are unable to differentiate between their viewpoint and that of others.[10] They assume everyone thinks and sees things just as they do. Like Kara, they use their new information with great satisfaction without checking to see whether they have figured things out correctly.

Preschool children also demonstrate their egocentric perspective in their belief that everyone and everything is like them. They think of inanimate objects as alive. The two- and three-year-olds in Sue's

Sunday school class loved the new puppet. When she began to stuff it into a bag, the children became upset. "No, he doesn't want to be in the bag," they protested. To the children, the puppet was not just cloth and plastic, so Sue had to find a special seat on a shelf for their new puppet friend. Stories of trees, flowers, or animals talking are very believable to small children, because the objects are acting like them. Even God is understood through their actions and experiences.

When four-year-old Nicky was asked how God answers prayer, he responded, "I don't know. Well, the Holy Spirit runs down and gets my prayers and takes them back to God." It made sense to him that the Holy Spirit would do things just as he does. What other way is there? Also note that Nicky had never asked how God hears prayer. He had been told God does hear prayer and simply assimilated that information without question, not sensing a need to know how God did it.

The egocentrism of young children is also evident in their conversation. Preschoolers love to talk to themselves. As they play alone they often carry on a continuous monologue, using their newly acquired language to express their imaginary activities. In analyzing the conversations of children playing together, Piaget found that until about the age of seven they often seem to be talking to themselves in the presence of others, engaging in what Piaget called *collective monologue*. They do not exchange ideas in conversation; rather, they simply make their own statements without wondering what others think. They do not try to take the perspective of another or attempt to understand the other person's point of view from what he or she says.

Another purpose of conversation in a group of preschool or early elementary children is to move others to some shared action.[11] Eavesdropping on Julie and Christie as they played house one afternoon, I heard Julie direct her sister, "I'll say, 'Mother, may I have a plum?' and you say, 'Yes, my darling.'" Four-year-old Julie was playing out her own story, using conversation to bring six-year-old Christie into her imaginary activity. Without realizing that Christie might have other ideas on how to play mother, Julie instructed Christie on how to act out her monologue with her.

Intuitive Logic

Young children use intuition rather than adult logic when they think. They simply internalize their perceptions and activities as mental pictures of their experiences. They do not coordinate their pieces of experiential knowledge by making rational or logical connections between the pieces.[12] Because they do not make those connections, but, rather, focus on each piece of learning, they are not troubled by ideas that, to the adult mind, are in conflict.

For example, young children tend to choose as their favorite Bible stories some of the dramatic Old Testament events such as David and Goliath, or Daniel in the lions' den. They are comforted by hearing that evil, dangerous people get punished. The fact that God loves everyone is also comforting to children. Adult logic demands that the love of God and the evidence that God punishes must be reconciled. Logical thinkers seek for a way to understand the character of God that explains the relationship between love and punishment. Young children usually are not ready to labor over those relationships. They are satisfied with their pieces of knowledge in the form of much-loved stories about God in action. Later they will need to work out the connections, but not during early childhood, except in the case of some very gifted children.

The connections young children do make are often the result of intuitive leaps rather than logical processing. As we have seen, words that sound alike may be connected and assumed to have the same meaning, or an activity appropriate in one setting may be incorporated into others. "When you get to climb a ladder, you say 'Bingo!'" Tammy announced confidently. Bingo was a word to be used not just in the game of Bingo but in Chutes and Ladders and all other games, whether it fit logically or not.

Sensorimotor Knowing

Piaget's observations of children led him to believe that they are frequently more advanced in action than they are in language and logical thought.[13] They can take action that they cannot describe in words and of which they apparently do not have a clear mental image. One way Piaget tested this belief was by giving children small objects such as houses, churches, and streets to construct the route they took on the way to school. Although they regularly found their way to school with ease, the young children were unable to describe or to construct the route using the objects provided. Before children can think logically, they must have a mental representation or a picture of events. Even before the mental representations are in place, however, children absorb a great deal at the action level.[14] They learn to find their way around neighborhoods, they figure out how to ride a bicycle, and they can reenact a story with the figures the teacher used to tell it.

In the preoperational stage, the child's motor memory is very effective. Children remember the things they do; they process concepts in action form that they cannot work with using only thought.[15] Children are also very good at remembering words. Adults often assume that if children know the words, they understand their meaning and can think with them.[16] Even though young children may have developed a large vocabulary, they still need to process concepts actively. Their logical thinking processes are still limited.

Irreversible Thinking

One of the major limitations is what Piaget calls *irreversibility*. Young children are perception bound. They believe what they see at the moment without thinking back over the process and without understanding the final state in light of what had led up to the moment.

Piaget's conservation experiments demonstrate the irreversible character of thinking. Children are shown two identical glasses containing equal amounts of colored water. After agreeing that the amount of liquid in glasses A and B is the same, the children are shown a taller, thinner glass (C) and are asked if, when the water in glass A is poured into glass C, the water in C and B will be the same. Children agree that the amount of liquid will be the same and watch as the water is poured into glass C. But when they see the higher water level in glass C, young children claim that it contains more water than B. In spite of their earlier affirmation, what they see changes their minds. They are unable to work backwards logically—reverse their thinking—and are unable to reason that if the amounts in A and B were the same, and they saw the content of A being poured into C, then C and B have to be the same.

The attention of young children centers on one thing at a time; what they see now seems to block out what they saw just a moment ago. Their attention is grasped by either height or width, but they do not consider both together to realize that increased height compensates for decreased width. They remember what they understood from what they saw.[17] They will remember that the amount of liquid changed, because, as they centered on one aspect of the final state, that is what they understood to be true. This experiment is a concrete example of how young children think; they focus on one thing at a time and do not perceive the whole process. They are strongly influenced by what they see and the meaning they make of that.

Children's Questions

One way to gain insight into the thinking of children and what is important to them is by listening to their questions. Toddlers begin with "What is it?" questions as they learn about the objects in their world. Around the age of three, "Why?" becomes an important question and increases in importance over the next three years. For adults, "why" may relate to either the goal or the cause of an action. But when young children ask "Why?" they want to know *both* the cause and the goal or the reason for the action. They have a sense that there is a cause and a purpose for everything.[18]

Around the age of four, children begin asking about origins. They are fascinated with the beginnings of living things, especially babies. They also become aware of death at this time and may have many questions about it. Their questions about death may alert us to their fear of death, which needs serious, assuring responses.

Children between the ages of four and six are full of questions. Parents and teachers can demonstrate respect for children by taking their questions seriously. Children deserve responses that give them satisfying information without overloading them with unnecessary and incomprehensible complexity. The answers should also be ones adults can respect as containing an adequate piece of the truth.

Children will challenge us with their questions. We may feel inadequate and be afraid to try to answer them. However, the fact that we take questions seriously and attempt an answer is more important than the perfection of the answer. When stymied by a child's question, we can ask, "What do you think?"[19] The child's response may give a good answer to affirm, or it may provide additional clues regarding what the child really wants to know and thus point us toward an adequate answer. As we honestly consider children's questions about life, death, and God, we too will learn and grow.

Concrete Operations or Concrete Intellectual Operations

Around the age of seven or eight, children make a major developmental breakthrough. Changes occur in the way they process intellectual matters, their affections, social relationships, and individual activities. These changes become possible as children discover that other people have viewpoints different from their own. They drop the limitation of being aware of no perspective but their own and begin to watch and listen to others to understand what they think and how they see things. When they know their perspective is one among many, they can question their own thinking and identify misunderstandings.

Children are then capable of reflection; they can conduct an internal discussion with themselves before they act. With this internal discussion, children can begin to consider the perspectives of others and the possible consequences of actions. Elementary-age children are no longer limited to trial and error in learning. Their ability to concentrate when working alone increases. They can cooperate with others on a task and can enter into discussions that are more than collective monologues, in which information and ideas are shared. Group games where children understand and are mutually committed to the rules become important in the lives of many middle to late elementary children.[20]

Logical Thinking

Seven- and eight-year-olds begin to think logically rather than intuitively. According to Piaget, logic is the mental processing that makes it possible to coordinate a series of perceptions and to blend them with intuitive knowledge while coordinating the viewpoints of different individuals. Thinking logically involves considering, connecting, and coordinating the perspectives of a variety of persons. It calls for reflecting on and possibly reorganizing experiences that were assimilated through intuition but never connected. Piaget refers to the process of logical thought as an operation. The mind acts—operates— on perceptions and information, coordinating them and transforming them from isolated pieces into parts of larger concepts.[21]

The mental process used during middle childhood is called *concrete operations*. Children think logically, but they think about concrete things. They think about actual objects, events, or commands that they could act out, but they are unable to process concepts that can be represented only in words.[22]

Reversible Thinking

Logical processes are possible after seven or eight years of age because children are able to reverse their thinking. Internally, they can look back to the beginning point of an experiment and consider each step of the process as well as the end result. Misunderstandings created by centering their attention on the end product are corrected when they can focus on each part of the whole process—when they can decenter.[23] In Piaget's conservation experiments, children with concrete operational mental abilities can reason that since no water has been lost, glasses C and B must have equal amounts of liquid in spite of appearances. They can also coordinate height and width, discovering what causes the difference in appearance.

Time Concepts

In this period of life, children begin to master the concept of time. By the age of seven or eight, children have developed a working understanding of calendar time and clock time. During the period of concrete operations, children learn to place events in sequential order with a duration of time inserted between them.[24] A time line would provide a picture of the sequential ordering of events for later elementary children. However, they may be adolescents before they truly comprehend historical or future time.[25]

Middle childhood is a period of significant development not only cognitively but also in the areas of relationships, will, and respect.[26] These areas will be explored in the next chapter on moral development.

Formal Operations or Abstract Intellectual Operations

As children move toward adolescence, eleven- or twelve-year-olds begin using new forms of thought and by the age of fourteen or fifteen may be quite skilled in what Piaget called *formal operations*—or logic.[27] The minds of these young teens begin to explore the world of ideas and philosophies. They are able to think about thoughts, even if those ideas have no concrete form, and to begin to build their conclusions into theories.[28] Midteens learn new methods of thinking to apply when exploring a wide range of different topics.[29] From reflection on several situations, young people can identify a common principle that may be built into a theory or a philosophy of life or used in problem solving. When faced with a problem, they can generate a range of possible solutions and are not bound only to the responses they have seen work in the past.

Formal or abstract logic does not just suddenly appear; rather, it develops out of experience with concrete logic. As they move into adolescence, children begin to apply to the realm of abstract thought the logical abilities they developed through working with concrete thoughts.[30] It is important to note, however, that although the potential for abstract thinking is released in many teenagers, some people go through life never becoming comfortable with thinking abstractly. Research into learning style preferences and personality differences suggests that some people, even though they can use abstract thinking, prefer to gather data from concrete experiences and to test the validity of ideas through active experimentation.[31] In spite of preferences, it is important that individuals are not trapped in concrete thinking but develop the ability to think abstractly and to be able to grasp realities that go beyond the concrete.

CAUSES OF DEVELOPMENT

Piaget was not satisfied with simply describing the characteristics of children's thinking; he also wanted to understand what caused development. He identified four factors: the biological factor of heredity and maturation, direct experience, social interaction, and the process of equilibration.[32] No one of these factors is sufficient to explain development; all of them are necessary.

Heredity and Maturation

Heredity and maturation provide the potential for development. Piaget did not mean by *heredity* that persons are preprogrammed for learning to automatically unfold within the child. Instead, he believed persons are born with a brain, which naturally engages with the world around them, taking in perceptions, organizing and making sense of them. As the brain matures it is able to organize information in new, more adequate ways, making possible qualitative changes in the child's thinking. Since in all children the biological capabilities mature in the same order, we see a predictable sequence in the stages of cognitive development.[33] The speed of development varies because of differences in the developmental timetables of children, but the sequence does not vary. Biological factors set the stage, but other factors must be in place if the intellectual potential of a child is to be realized.

Direct Experience

Children need direct experience with the physical world if they are going to develop cognitively. As they encounter objects, handle and interact with them, they discover the characteristics of the objects and also learn about the effect of their actions on them. Young children can amuse themselves for a long time manipulating commonplace things.

As we talked by the punch bowl while guests were leaving the reception, Towanna kept an eye on her four-year-old daughter. All the time we were talking, Michelle amused herself by pulling into a neat, tight square the chairs guests had left scattered around the room. Intermittently she worked and then studied the results of her labors. From such activities children may be learning concepts that adults cannot remember learning.

Piaget gives the example of a boy playing with pebbles. The boy arranged the pebbles in a straight line and counted them, using the skill he had recently learned. Then, he placed them side by side in a line that was shorter and counted them again. After arranging the pebbles in a circle, he counted them a third time, discovering the fact that no matter how he arranged them, the number of pebbles stayed constant. This is a significant new concept for the child.[34] Children learn and develop as they experience the objects around them.

Social Interaction

The social environment also influences the development of children. The actualization of the child's developmental potential is enhanced or retarded by the richness or poverty of his or her social interaction.[35] We saw earlier that the egocentric perspective of young children keeps them from questioning their thinking and from discovering misunderstandings. Piaget found that interaction with other children is the major means whereby young children are released from their egocentric perspectives.[36] As they play together and solve relational problems, they become aware that other children see things differently, and they begin to compare their views with those of others. They must rearrange the structures of their thinking to accommodate the new discoveries, and as they do so, development occurs.

Children pick up new pieces of information and perspectives as they interact with adults and other children. The new understandings may be in conflict with the old ones, thus requiring the child to substitute new ideas for old ones. In other cases they integrate ideas in new ways, bringing them into harmony.

Equilibration

Some educators believe that all learning and change can be explained by external influences and by the impact the external environment of events and people has on the child.[37] But Piaget's research indicated that the sequence of stages in cognitive development is the same for children in very different environments. He concluded, therefore, that environment alone could not explain development.[38] The inner factors of heredity and maturation, along with what Piaget called equilibration, are at work coordinating the other factors and causing development.[39]

The process goes something like this: As the brain matures, children become aware of new realities through experience and in social interaction, discovering perspectives they never noticed before. When the new information is different from their understandings, or they discover that some of the things they assimilated into a mental category do not fit, inner conflict or disequilibration occurs. Human beings are born with the need to resolve those inner conflicts and restore equilibrium; they make the changes in their thinking that are necessary to reestablish harmony and a sense of adequacy. This is the process of equilibration at work—the motor of development.[40]

FACILITATING DEVELOPMENT

Children are always learning from all their experiences and relationships. What they learn in the formal setting of elementary school or Sunday school is only a small portion of their discoveries. Everyday life is the setting for the most powerful educational experiences and relationships.[41] The way in which parents, adult friends, and teachers cooperate with the necessary causes of development makes a big difference in whether the child's experiences lead to positive learning and development. By applying Piaget's theory, adults can assist in releasing the developmental potential of children through accepting heredity and maturation, providing for direct experience, encouraging social interaction, and supporting equilibration.

Accepting Heredity and Maturation

We have shown that each child's heredity and rate of maturation are givens, which cannot be changed. However, the way in which significant adults in a child's life relate to those givens does influence learning and development. It is important that we accept each child's developmental timetable and uniqueness in all areas. Knowing the sequence of cognitive development helps us not only to accept but also to celebrate what is normal, healthy development during each stage. When we are aware of what is normal, we will not fret but, instead, allow for those normal limitations, major on the strengths of the child's thought processes, and wait patiently for the readiness that prepares for new discoveries.

During the sensorimotor phase, babies need objects and toys to manipulate, and they need acceptance of their experimentation, even when it means repeatedly picking up a dropped toy. Our patience may be increased by realizing that the baby is not being ornery but is practicing a new discovery—when things are dropped over the side of the high chair, they go down.

Since children between the ages of two and eight enjoy discovering new pieces of information, this is an excellent time to provide them with a rich supply of stories. From stories they can learn about nature, relationships, and God, and they can get to know the characters of the Bible. You can find these stories in books written for children of all ages, which are available in a wide range of topics. As you tell stories, read to children, and help them build books into their lives as friends, remember that children enjoy the individual stories without struggling to connect them all. They probably will not be able to retell the stories in words, but they do enjoy and learn them. They can review stories using figures to act out the events and in time will be able to tell the story in words.

Pictures inform and help focus the attention of perception-bound young children. They like to look at pictures as they listen to stories; a picture of Jesus in a child's room can be a visible reminder of his presence with them. Children watch many hours of pictures on television and video, which may be very instructive, but young children can also be disturbed by what they see. Pictures have a powerful impact on children, and it is important for parents to know what they are seeing. Children need the support and reassurance of parents when they have seen something that troubles them.

Since the minds of young children center on one thing at a time, they may focus on one part of a story and miss the point the adult thought was important. Sometimes children's fears connect with a certain piece of a story. In the story of Samuel, for instance, a child may focus on the fact that Hannah left Samuel at the tabernacle and may hear nothing more because of the fear that he or she might be left at church. Adults working with children must be alert to evidence that a child may have focused on something that is causing fear and provide the comfort needed.

More often, however, the piece of the story that catches the attention of children relates to a need they are processing. When working with the parable of the Good Shepherd, six-year-old Katie constructed a sheepfold on her sheet of paper and filled it with cotton-ball sheep; eight-year-old Jordan acted out the story with laminated figures on a felt underlay. The Good Shepherd wrestled with the wolf and won. Katie focused on the safety of the sheepfold, Jordan on the victorious strength of the Good Shepherd. They each needed to process a different piece of the story, and the centering of their minds served them well in leading them to do that.

Also note that Jordan, on the threshold of concrete operations, had concrete objects to use as he thought about the Good Shepherd. With those figures he expressed thoughts that went beyond what the teacher had included in the story. Jordan was beginning to construct his concept of the Good Shepherd. He did not have to wait until he could think abstractly to do that; he could begin at age eight to build concrete pieces for his concept of the Good Shepherd.

Americans value speed; we tend to assume that faster is always better. However, in the area of development, children are not best served by parents and teachers bent on the maximum acceleration of mental growth. Such efforts may lead to frustration, memorization of words without grasping concepts, and even a sense of inadequacy on the part of the children when they cannot grasp what we try to teach them. Children need from us a rich, accepting environment in which they can learn and grow at the pace that is best for them.[42]

Providing for Direct Experience

Piaget believed that more than words from adults are needed to bring about change and cognitive development in children. Discoveries made through direct experiences are more transformational and exciting for children than lessons in which adults tell them what they ought to know. This does not mean that adults should never pass on to children important information. It does mean, however, that we should not depend on the telling method as our main contribution to the child's development.

Play is one form of experience that enhances a child's development. When children play, they are not putting in time with meaningless activity; play is their work. As they enter into the experiences of dramatic play, children act out what they will later internalize as thoughts. David Elkind says that "what children acquire through active manipulation of the environment is nothing less than the ability to think."[43] In other words, through play children actively think things through.

Children benefit greatly from the freedom to play creatively. Elaborate toys are not needed for creative play. As a matter of fact, too many toys may be distracting. Children can find days of enjoyment playing in a large cardboard box or in a tent made from an old blanket. They need a place where they are free to manipulate things without the fear of breaking something and being punished. Providing children with adequate time for play is also important and calls for managing the amount of television they watch. When given large blocks of time for play, children learn to create their own enjoyment and to exercise their imagination, releasing them from dependence on others to entertain them. Young children can profit from times of free play not only at home but also during their time at church.

Children who play outdoors have opportunity to discover the wonder of God's creation. Regular visits to a park or a nature preserve are important for city children living in apartments or with limited backyard space. Church-sponsored day camps and residential camps can enrich the lives of children.

Parents and faith communities have values they believe are important to pass on to their children, and children are most likely to understand and eventually own those values if they have the opportunity to experience them. When we prepare to teach a value, we must begin by asking how we can lead children to experience the value; later we may ask how we can best talk about the value. As we saw in chapter 3, parents can assist children in building a firm foundation for faith—trust—in God by giving them the experience of parents who can be trusted. Children can learn love and respect for older people by going to a senior citizens' home to sing for or play games with the residents, or a Sunday school class could adopt a grandmother or grandfather and do special things for her or him throughout the year. Through each experience children learn Christian values.

Stories and their meaning will be learned best by children if they actively experience them. One way this can be done is to have the children act out the story together after first listening to it. Very young children like to play the same part; they can all be Zacchaeus pretending to climb the tree, wait for Jesus, and climb down to take Jesus home to dinner. Older children like to take separate parts, supplying the words of the story or pantomiming the story as it is read. Children profit from taking figures used in presenting a story and telling it again to themselves as they act it out—experiencing it through the figures.

When children are learning from their experiences, they want to repeat the activities. Repetition gives them mental exercise and helps them master what they are learning.[44] Learning-activity materials presented in Sunday school should be available to children for several weeks, allowing them to choose from three or four options the activity that is most meaningful to them. Story figures for a unit of study could be placed in a story center where children could work with whichever stories they choose.

Choice is important to children's learning. Jean Piaget and Maria Montessori, an expert in early childhood education, found that an inner motivation to learn grew within children when they were able to choose the activities they wanted to work with and when they had blocks of time that allowed them to become totally engrossed in the activity.[45] Children not only learn much from immersion in experience, they also come to love learning.

Encouraging Social Interaction

Another way in which parents and teachers facilitate development is by providing opportunities for and encouraging children to interact with others. There are several ways through which this can happen. Children who attend day-care centers or who are in school mix with children their own age every day, but some children are limited in their opportunities for interaction with other children unless their parents intentionally expand their contacts. Some parents send children to preschool two or three half-days a week to give them more time with children their age. Another approach is for families to regularly invite children into the home to be with their child.

Children benefit not only from interaction with their peers but also from developing friendships with older or younger children, teenagers, and adults. The church is the institution with the greatest potential for providing children, youth, and adults with enriching intergenerational friendships in addition to peer-group relationships. In America, where individualism is glorified, and we try to make the nuclear family sufficient unto itself, the potential for intergenerational friendships will not be realized unless church leaders intentionally plan to release it. Parents who are at a distance from their relatives can create an extended family by regularly inviting adopted grandparents, aunts and uncles, or another family with children to do things with their family.

In formal Christian education settings, teachers sometimes discourage conversation between children, preferring to have the children respond mainly to the teacher who is in control. For the most effective learning, however, children need to interact with their classmates as well as the teacher. Informal times for getting acquainted with each other are important for children whose only connection is through the church. They will learn from each other as they work on cooperative projects and as older children discuss what they are learning and doing.

By being with parents and other adults as they go about the activities of their daily lives, children learn things without realizing they are learning. Five-year-old Cathy walked across the street, knocked on the door, and announced to the woman of the house, whom she had never seen before, "I've come to visit." Cathy's father was a pastor beginning his ministry in a new town by spending the morning visiting some of his church members. Wanting to be just like Daddy, Cathy had set out on her own ministry by calling on the elderly lady who over the next several years enjoyed the friendship of her little visitor. Cathy told me this story as we discussed the ministry skills she had learned by being alongside her parents as they did ministry. Children learn basic values and skills, and their development is enhanced when parents and adult friends include them in life events. By watching adults interact, they learn.

Parents in this technological age face a challenge with which earlier generations did not have to deal. Many children are fascinated by television, video games, and computers. If they are allowed to, some children will spend many hours a day in front of the television or the computer screen. This deprives them of social interaction and may hinder their development. Parents need to set limits on the amount of time their children spend with the television or the computer and to invest more time interacting with their children and giving them opportunities to interact with others.

Supporting Equilibration

Equilibration, the motor of development, is an inner process that parents and teachers cannot control. Most of the time children manage the process with relative ease, but children may be faced with issues they have difficulty equilibrating. In those times we can support children in their disequilibration and inner struggle.

One of the best ways to assist children with the equilibration process is to value their questions, letting them know that they can bring to us any confusing or troubling question and it will be treated with respect. Over time, our responsiveness to common questions prepares the way for children to trust us with the troubling questions. Listen for comments or questions that might indicate that children are experiencing disquiet or inner turmoil.

Every few nights over several weeks, Janelle would crawl into bed, cuddle close to her mother, and express her fear that her mother would die. She was struggling to fit ideas and fears about death into her understandings. Patiently Lisa held her little daughter, comforted her, and stretched her own understanding of death and God's love as she talked with Janelle in response to her questions. In time, peace returned and the issue was laid to rest. Probably Janelle will continue to develop her understanding of death later, but for the time, with her mother's help, equilibration was restored.

Learning is an ongoing process that involves learning, unlearning, and relearning.[46] During childhood there is no way to avoid learning that is incomplete and contains misunderstandings. But in the early, incomplete learning of children there are critical pieces of reality. Out of their concrete knowing will flow the ability to comprehend the heart of the matter. At every stage of development, the way of knowing is critical to an eventual mature knowing and deserves to be highly valued.

Five

THE CHILD'S VIEW
ON RIGHT AND WRONG

ndrew handed me a plastic container and then stood with his mother, waiting for me to open it and discover my treat—two mincemeat tarts his daddy, Don, had baked. After I expressed my appreciation for this special gift, Lenore asked her four-year-old son, "Can you tell Miss Cathy why we brought the tarts?" Andrew twisted on one foot, hung his head for a few seconds, then, looking up with a shy smile answered, "Because she likes us." "Well, yes, we are glad she likes us," Lenore responded, looking just a little embarrassed, "and we like her too, don't we?"

This brief event gave me a glimpse into both Andrew's moral education and his moral development. Instead of bringing the tarts herself, Lenore involved Andrew in this act of sharing the love of their family with another. She was giving her son experience with a family value, which we have seen is important for a child's development. Apparently, while preparing the package of tarts, mother and son had talked about the reason for giving the gift. The reason, however, had been adjusted to fit the thinking of a normal four-year-old child who sees everything from one perspective, his own.

For Don and Lenore, like many Christian parents, the moral development of their son is very important. They know God calls people to live in love and justice, to think and to do what is right. How can they help Andrew learn to decide what is right and to have the strength to do what he knows to be right?

As Jean Piaget studied children, he discovered that they were moral philosophers who struggled with good and evil, understanding and applying rules. In the 1930s Piaget began to study the moral development of children, focusing on three- to eleven-year-olds. Lawrence Kohlberg discovered the work of Piaget and, building on that work, continued the study of moral development. Initially, he studied the moral reasoning of ninety-eight American boys, ages ten to sixteen. For over thirty years he interviewed those boys every three years to see how their moral reasoning had changed over time. He also did moral development research in other cultures.[1] Out of his extensive study, Kohlberg and his colleagues developed and refined an understanding of moral development.

Often the focus of moral education given by parents and teachers in the church is on moral actions. We want children to do what is right, and we believe that will happen if we teach them what is right. Researchers, however, have found that children who had religious education or character education classes were no less likely to cheat, lie, or steal than were the children who had not had moral instruction classes.[2] Apparently teaching children what is right or wrong is not sufficient to guarantee that children will act on what they have been taught is moral.

Piaget and Kohlberg discovered that when children are faced with a moral decision, their thinking processes differ from the moral reasoning of most adults. They also found that the structures—the form or process—of moral reasoning develop in a pattern of sequential stages. To understand why children act as they do and to know how to help them to develop morally, we need to understand the way in which they think about moral questions at each stage.

Insights from Piaget and Kohlberg can help us understand what is going on inside children as they deal with the moral challenges of everyday life. In this chapter we will examine the moral reasoning of children, consider how adults can encourage the moral development of children, and also explore the factors Piaget and Kohlberg believed make a difference in whether children translate moral reasoning into moral action. A third scholar, Robert Coles, has also studied the moral life of children. This chapter closes with an examination of Coles's reflections about children faced with extraordinary moral challenges.

THE PATTERN OF MORAL DEVELOPMENT

From extensive research, Kohlberg identified three levels of moral reasoning and two stages within each level. As he interviewed people, listening to them think out loud about moral dilemmas, he traced changes in the way each person understood and used various moral values and perspectives and was able to assess their level of moral development. Seeing how some of these values and perspectives develop can help us better understand the moral thinking of children. Table 2 outlines the sequence of changes in a person's understanding of the following aspects of moral reasoning: source of authority, definition of right and wrong, motivation to do the right and avoid the wrong, consideration of intentions, ability to take the perspective of others, the value of persons, and understanding justice. Since stages one, two, and three are the stages of childhood, we will explore them the most fully.

Level I

Although younger children simply act spontaneously without thinking about what is right or wrong,[3] by the age of four or five, children begin making moral judgments using reasons similar to those employed by other children their age.[4] Children under the age of nine can be expected to use level I moral reasoning, and some may continue in this level longer.[5]

Source of Authority

During level I, self-interest is the source of moral authority. As noted in the last chapter, Piaget discovered that young children are bound in their egocentric perspective or point of view.

Stage 1. At stage 1, young children think they are obeying rules laid down by their parents, but they act based on their own interpretation

Table 2
Kohlberg's Levels of Moral Reasoning

Egocentric - - - - - - - - - - - - - - - - ▶ Perspectivistic

	Level I	Level II	Level III
	Self-Interest	External Standards—Models and Rules	Internal Principles
Source of Authority	What adults command. Later, equal treatment.	Defined by society.	Equal consideration for all.
Definitions	Right is what adults command or what brings reward. Wrong is what I am punished for—what brings pain.	Right is what good people do or what the law says one should do. Wrong is what good people do not do or what the law says one should not do.	Right is living out moral principles and being just. Wrong is violating a moral principle and being unjust.
Stimulus to Right Actions	Fear of punishment and desire for reward.	Desire to please important persons and perform one's duty to society.	To be true to oneself one must act upon the moral principles to which one is committed.
Intentions	Oblivious to intentions.	Makes allowances for intentions. Lenience tempered by sense of duty.	Considers intentions but also concerned about justice.
Ability to Take Another's Perspective	Understands the perspective of persons in situations that he or she has experienced.	Understands the perspective of friends, family, and eventually society.	Understands the perspective of a wide range of persons, including minority groups.
Value of Persons	Valued in material terms. Persons are valuable for what they do for *me*.	Valued because of relationships of affection and for their contribution to society.	Valued because they are persons. Human life is sacred.
Justice	What adults command. Later, equal treatment.	Defined by society.	Equal consideration for all.

Table developed by Catherine Stonehouse, Orlean Bullard Professor of Christian Education at Asbury Theological Seminary.

of the rules. They are unaware of what they do not understand about the rules.[6] When playing games, they may state rules they have heard older children discuss and then go ahead with the game, contentedly playing it just as they want to and letting others do the same. In the end, everyone wins.[7]

Stage 2. Around the age of seven or eight, children begin to break away from their egocentric viewpoint. They want to play with other children and coordinate their play using rules, which they still understand only vaguely. No longer are they satisfied with everyone winning; each person wants to be the sole winner.[8] At this point they are moving into stage 2 moral reasoning. What is good for *me* becomes the ultimate moral authority. Situations are judged good or bad depending on whether the individual's needs and interests are met. At level I, children do not understand the need for a source outside themselves that gives authority to moral decisions.

Defining Right and Wrong

The child using level I moral reasoning thinks of right and wrong in external terms; there are good and bad actions and events, but the child is unaware of good or bad standards or persons.[9] Young children judge rightness and wrongness based on the physical or self-gratifying consequences of an act.[10]

Stage 1. For young children during stage 1, right is obeying the commands of parents and other authorities and avoiding punishment. Wrong is an act that results in punishment or physical damage.[11] Through experiencing the rewards and the punishment that result from their actions, children discover what the authorities in their world label as right and wrong. They attach the labels to the specific acts for which they have been rewarded or punished and do not grasp the generalized applications to similar situations, which adults assume they will make.

Young children believe that the greater the amount of physical damage, the greater the wrong. In his research, Piaget used stories to help children share their moral reasoning with him. He told about a boy whose mother called him for dinner. Obediently the boy came quickly and pushed open the dining room door, not knowing that fifteen cups sat on a tray behind the door. The door hit the tray, all fifteen cups fell to the floor and broke. Another boy, while his mother was out, climbed up on a chair and reached high into the cupboard trying to get a jar of jam. Stretching for the jam, he knocked one cup out of the cupboard, which fell onto the floor and broke. At the end of the stories, Piaget asked, "Which of these children was naughtiest? Why?" Young children responded, "The boy who broke fifteen cups is naughtiest. Fifteen is more than one."[12]

This reasoning of young children also applies to judging the wrongness of lies; they think the story furthest from the truth is the worst.[13] The attention of young children focuses on the *quantity* of falsehood. They do not realize that the story closer to the truth is likely to be more believable, and therefore, more deceptive. Quantity is what impresses them, whether it is quantity of damage or of falsehood.

Children listen to and observe adults and older children as they go about their lives. From their words and actions, young children pick up many rules that they build into their view of right and wrong.[14] One evening after I had visited with a family, the five-year-old son stood watching as his father began to help me put on my coat. With distress in his voice he said, "Daddy, don't do that. She's not your wife." His observations had led him to believe it was right for a man to hold a coat only for his wife. Parents may be unaware of rules that worry their young children.

Stage 2. At stage 2, right is what serves one's personal interests and needs. Right is also a fair deal where two people receive equal, concrete benefits.[15] Wrong is when things do not work out to the person's advantage or when not all people are treated equally. Parents often hear reports of wrong from their children: "He took the last cookie, and I didn't get one." Or, "Her piece of cake is bigger than mine." Strict equality is necessary for things to be right at stage 2.

If the chances are good of getting away with an action without being punished, the stage 2 person judges it to be okay. The self-serving focus of stage 2 is disturbing to parents and teachers, but it is a normal portion of the moral development path—a time when many children do take risks and discover the consequences of their actions.

Motivation to Do Right

Stage 1. Young children do what is right because they believe they ought to obey their parents and others in authority. The child's first moral feelings involve a sense that it is right to obey; children also want to avoid punishment. The desire to obey and to avoid punishment causes children to accept rules of conduct long before they are able to understand why the actions are right or wrong.[16]

When children first begin trying to obey, they tend to be concerned about obedience only when the authority is present. One afternoon, five-year-old Paul rode his new bicycle to a park a few blocks from home—something he had been told not to do. When his mother discovered he had been to the park alone, she was concerned. "Why did you go to the park when Mommy told you not to?" she asked. "I didn't think you would know," he responded. At that point in his moral development, Mother's commands carried weight with Paul only when she was physically present.[17] If Mother would not know he had gone to the park, as he assumed, there would be no punishment to avoid and, therefore, no need to obey the rule.

Kohlberg believed the young child's conscience is mainly fear of punishment.[18] If there is no punishment to fear, conscience does not control behavior. The fear may be irrational—not stimulated by dire threats from parents but the product of the child's mind and imagination.

Stage 2. Children in stage 2 are motivated to do what is right to gain rewards and benefits. The desire for reward tends to outweigh their fear of punishment. Sometimes they look at punishment pragmatically. If the potential reward is great enough, they may choose to go ahead and do what they want, willing to pay the price of being punished to gain the desired reward.[19] Children differ on how tenaciously they go after what they want and how willing they are to risk punishment. What they find rewarding or punishing will also vary from child to child. These individual differences call for thoughtful responses from parents and teachers.

Awareness of Intentions

Stage 1. Adults are often surprised to discover that young children are blind to intentions and the role they play in moral actions.[20] When Nicky was told Piaget's story of the boys who broke the cups, he quickly declared, "The boy who broke fifteen was naughtiest." As the interviewer quizzed Nicky further, he thought hard for a few moments, then changed his decision. "The boy who broke one cup was the worst." At first it seemed that Nicky was using moral reasoning beyond what was expected of a four-year-old child. But his final comment indicated his thinking process. "He did more; he did two things. He broke the cup, and he disobeyed his mom." Nicky did not count the boy who broke fifteen cups less guilty because he was intending to be obedient and simply had an accident. His decision was still based on quantity of wrong done, not on intention.

Stage 2. Kohlberg found that in stage 2 moral reasoning, the attention is totally focused on whether personal interests are being served.[21] Stage 2 children are not thinking about intentions or reflecting on whether their self-interest is right. They understand the intentions of self-interest but do not move beyond that.

Taking the Perspective of Others

The ability or inability to put oneself in the shoes of another greatly influences moral reasoning. Moral development requires the ability to take the perspective—understand the point of view—of an ever expanding number of people.[22]

Stage 1. Young children, as we have seen, are unaware of perspectives different from their own. They do not, therefore, ask how others feel or what they want in a given situation. Even as they begin to realize that others do not think as they do, they focus on the physical consequences of actions and are unaware of the psychological interests and needs of others. In obedience to family or classroom rules, they may avoid causing physical harm but have no concern for the psychological pain they inflict on another.

Tammy and her cousin Paul—four and a half and three years old respectively—sat coloring at the table. Tammy refused to let her brother Ted join in the coloring. Even though Ted was four days older than Paul, he developed on a timetable slightly slower than Paul's. Ted did not yet have the small muscle coordination needed to color inside the lines well enough to satisfy Tammy. Feeling excluded, Ted protested by attacking the other children with his fists. Tammy and Paul ran off with no sense of guilt; Ted was the one in the wrong. If questioned, Tammy and Paul would have vehemently claimed, "We didn't do anything wrong. Ted hit us." They recognized the pain and wrongness of Ted's physical actions but were oblivious to the psychological pain they had caused by excluding Ted.

During stage 1 children also confuse the perspective of authorities with their own.[23] They interpret what they are told within their own frame of reference, fitting it into their way of thinking, and they expect adults to react to situations as they would. Parents who take intentions into consideration when judging their children's actions, may wonder why their youngsters are so fearful when, for example, they accidentally break something. Children do not realize that their parents will consider intentions. To the young child it is as bad to break a vase accidentally as it is to throw it down in anger and break it. They expect to be severely punished, but as parents treat them differently based on intentions, over time they, too, will begin considering intentions as they make moral judgments.

Stage 2. By the time children move into stage 2, they are aware that other individuals do have different perspectives and that interests often conflict. Their solution for resolving the dilemma of conflicting desires is equal exchange.[24] Elementary-age children keep careful records of whose turn it is to sit in the front seat when riding somewhere with Mom, who gets to choose which television show to watch, and whose turn it is to unload the dishwasher. They give to the other person what they judge to be fair in terms of concrete equality so that they can have their equal share. They do not realize that differences in age, ability, and personality are not well served by strict, concrete equality.

Since the thinking of elementary-age children is concrete, this limits their ability to take the perspective of others. They are able to understand the experiences of people like themselves who are in situations that they, too, have experienced. They are unable to empathize with people outside their small circle of experience.

The Value of Persons

Another important element in the way we reason morally is how we understand the value of persons. Why we value people changes as moral development takes place.

Stage 1. Children love their parents but also fear them. Out of this fear and affection is born the first moral awareness—unilateral respect—which causes children to value obedience and to think of adults as more important than children. A reality of life for young children is that they must literally look up to adults. The size and authority of adults (not just parents) impresses children and leads them to think of adults as superior to themselves, again resulting in unilateral respect. Children respect adults without expecting adults to respect them or realizing that other children might also be worthy of respect. An example of unilateral respect is seen in the attitude of young children toward lying. They believe it is wrong to lie to an adult but are not bothered by lying to another child.[25] When pushed to tell why persons are of value, young children talk in terms of physical worth and place higher value on people they think are important.[26]

Stage 2. Children at stage 2 value people for what they can do for them. They understand human value in terms of how people contribute to meeting the needs of others.[27] During the family vacation when Ted had been excluded from the coloring activities, he had faced another problem. His legs were shorter than Tammy's and Paul's, and he was always being left behind when the others ran off to play. Tammy had been having a wonderful time with cousin Paul, because he could more fully meet her needs as a playmate. Ted had not contributed as much to her fun that week as Paul had, and therefore Ted was less valued and left behind. Although Tammy was too young to articulate this reason for valuing a person, her experience was preparing her to value persons for what they could contribute to her enjoyment.

Understanding Justice

Justice is not a word heard often in the conversation of young children. They do, however, talk frequently about fairness, which is how they understand justice.

Stage 1. Preschool children tend to accept whatever adults demand as fair. Concrete rules, assumed to come from adult authorities, describe what is just or fair, and the rules are to be applied equally to everyone without exceptions for special needs. The only inequality that young children perceive as fair is when important people are given special treatment.[28]

When Piaget asked children what punishment would be fair for a child who had done something wrong, he was amazed by the severity of the punishment they prescribed. They seemed to believe severe punishment was just, at least when they were talking about it.[29] Young children also believe in imminent justice; they expect punishment automatically to follow a transgression, even when no one else knows about the misdeed.[30] At times when children have misbehaved, they need to receive some form of punishment to restore their inner sense of rightness. It seems that they need to feel that they have paid for the wrong to be able to move on.

Stage 2. Fairness, understood as strict, quantitative equality, is extremely important to children using stage 2 moral reasoning. If they do something for someone, they expect the person to do them an equal favor. That is fair.[31] To them, absolute equality is just. They do not comprehend the need to make allowances for a younger child or for an older sibling to have the privilege of staying up later unless they, too, receive some desired privilege.

Level II

Through their efforts to obey, to avoid punishment, and to work things out for their advantage, children discover in the world around them moral values that guide the lives of others. Children come to accept these values as their own and begin to use level II moral reasoning. Kohlberg labeled level II *conventional morality.* It is a period in which people live by the conventions—the accepted values—of their society. Later elementary or middle school children begin using level II moral reasoning. Most adolescents depend on level II reasoning, and some adults never move beyond this level.[32]

Source of Authority

At level II, external standards become the authority persons consult when making moral judgments or decisions. People are no longer locked in their fear of punishment or in their preoccupation with self-interest. They are now ready to explore the moral guidelines others have found helpful.

Stage 3. Children first understand external standards as they discover that family members, friends, and teachers are guided by certain values and have expectations for how people should act. Those expectations describe what good people do in various roles and settings. They become the standards to which the stage 3 child begins to conform.[33] Children watch friends, parents, other adults, and teenagers they admire to see how they do things. What they see becomes the pattern they try to follow. Parents often hear the claim, "Everyone's doing it," as children argue for some privilege. The fact that the activity is acceptable for their friends is viewed as evidence of an authoritative standard they feel their parents should consider when responding to their plea.

Stage 4. The laws of society provide moral authority at stage 4. Laws are made to order society for the good of everyone.[34] Laws are valued for the order they bring to society. Life runs much more smoothly when everyone follows the law as their source of authority.

Defining Right and Wrong

Stage 3. At this stage, right is being a good person by doing what a good son or daughter, brother or sister, student or friend is expected to do. Good people are believed to be concerned about others, to be loyal, respectful, and grateful, which identifies these attitudes as right for the stage 3 person.[35] Doing what the people we love and respect expect us to do is also right; wrong is breaking trust by failing to do what these important people expect us to do.

Stage 4. Obeying the law, doing one's duty, and contributing to society define what is right at stage 4.[36] Wrong is breaking the law or not accepting rightful responsibility in society.

Motivation to Do Right

Stage 3. Children in stage 3 want to be good. They want to think of themselves as good sons or daughters, friends, or team members, and the desire to be considered good motivates them to right actions. They also want to please those for whom they care. Anticipated disapproval will often keep a stage 3 child from doing wrong, whether the likelihood of the disapproval is real or imagined. Being liked is important to late elementary and middle school children. To be liked, they must avoid disapproval, and this motivates them to meet the expectations of those they are trying to please. They choose to be good or nice to preserve relationships.[37] When disciplining stage 3 children for negative behavior, parents and teachers can help them understand how certain behaviors harm relationships. Facing the relational consequences of their actions will often have more influence on their behavior than threats of punishment.

Stage 4. Maintaining order in society by obeying the law is what motivates stage 4 adolescents and adults to do what is right. As they grow in their understanding of the law and as their value for it increases, they commit themselves to obey the law, and it becomes a matter of personal conscience for them. They then obey the law to avoid a guilty conscience. They also want to be honored as a person who makes a contribution to society. The law and what it does for society is so important to stage 4 persons that they will obey the law even when there is little chance of being caught if they were to disobey it.[38]

Awareness of Intentions

Stage 3. In stage 3, intentions become an important factor in moral reasoning. For the first time, actions are judged good or bad based on the motives of the actor not just on the consequences of the act. At stage 3 motives are judged good or bad based on the motives a good person would be expected to have in the situation. Selfish motives, which predominated at stage 2, are no longer judged acceptable in stage 3 moral reasoning, which is concerned about others and about maintaining relationships. Good motives can even excuse bad consequences. Phrases such as, "He meant well," or, "She didn't mean to hurt anyone," often appear in the moral reasoning of this stage, which tends to be lenient with those who have acted unwisely but with good intentions.[39]

Stage 4. In the moral reasoning of stage 4 there is the awareness of intentions and the expectation that people must take responsibility for the outcome of their actions. An action that violates the law or is likely to cause harm is judged as wrong, even if motivated by good intentions. Stage 4 persons believe the law provides the best treatment for the most people and, therefore, law should guide actions, not personal good intentions.[40]

Taking the Perspective of Others

Stage 3. Although early elementary children may memorize the Golden Rule, they are unable to use it in moral reasoning until they reach stage 3. The Golden Rule requires that persons be able to think of themselves simultaneously in two roles: the person needing help and the person giving help. They must put themselves in the place of the other person, feeling what they feel, discerning what they expect and what they need. At the same time they ask, "What can I do to meet those needs and expectations?" During stage 3 the Golden Rule is applied concretely, identifying specific actions appropriate for particular individuals in specific situations. Stage 3 moral reasoning expands to take the perspective—understanding the viewpoint—of family and friends but does not grasp the perspective of those who are outside that circle.[41]

Stage 4. Persons using stage 4 moral reasoning take the perspective of the society. They judge individuals and groups in terms of how they fit into the society and of the contribution they make to it. What is best for society as a whole is the lens through which stage 4 persons view all events.[42]

The Value of Persons

Stage 3. At stage 2, persons were valued for the concrete things they could do for someone else. As children grow in their awareness of love and affection, their value of persons changes. At stage 3, they understand the worth of persons to be in the love and affection that bonds them to each other. They are valued for the love they give and the love others have for them. Family members and friends are more highly valued than others at this stage. When it comes to moral action, individuals are expected to take risks and sacrifice to help out family and friends but not to have obligations to others.[43]

Cooperation between children begins during stage 2 as they negotiate conflicts to serve the interests of each other. As children move into stage 3, out of that initial cooperation grows mutual respect—as they grasp that children, including themselves, are persons of worth to be respected as adults are respected. Once this respect for children develops, lying to a friend becomes as wrong as lying to adults. Children also realize that cheating in a game is a sign of disrespect for the other children and is therefore wrong.[44]

Stage 4. Life is considered sacred by those at stage 4 because it is declared sacred by society or religion, which requires the protection of life. Individuals are valued for the contribution they make to society, which may lead to the devaluing of the disabled, the poor, and the unemployed. Children may also be overlooked because they are not yet seen as contributors to society. Stage 4 moral reasoning often lacks concern for the needs and interests of minority groups, since the good of society as a whole, represented by the majority, is the prime value.[45]

Understanding Justice

Stage 3. Following the Golden Rule is just by stage 3 standards. Determining what is just requires that children think through in their imagination what each person needs and what each one can give in a particular situation. Fairness no longer requires strict, quantitative equality; instead, fairness takes into consideration the special needs of those who require more help. Justice does not demand an eye for an eye; a person may choose to forgive.[46]

Stage 4. Justice, in stage 4 moral reasoning, is what the laws of society declare as just using the procedures society has established for resolving conflict. It is just to apply the laws and procedures equally to all members in the society and unjust if exceptions are made. Since laws serve the whole society, stage 4 thinkers believe that it is fair to place the good of the majority—the good of society—above individual needs.[47]

Gender Considerations

As noted earlier in this chapter, the participants in Kohlberg's initial moral development study were all boys and men, although women and girls were included in later studies. Carol Gilligan, a colleague of Kohlberg, listened to the responses of women and girls in those later studies and noted that the issues they struggled with differed from the concerns of men. As she began to study the moral reasoning and development of girls and women, Gilligan saw a major change in girls as they entered adolescence, a change that did not take place in the moral development of boys. Girls, who at nine and eleven years of age had been honest about their feelings and beliefs, became unwilling to express their feelings and thoughts during early adolescence.[48] It seems that as girls enter level II in their moral development and become aware of the "good girl" image held by friends, family, and society, they try to conform to that image. In their efforts to be a "good girl," some hide their true feelings and thoughts and in time lose touch with their real self as they invest their energy in trying to please the people who are important to them.

Society's image of the "good girl" is someone who never confronts or leads, is not too intelligent, and does not disagree with what others believe or want to do. Many adolescent girls are squeezed into this mold, making them morally vulnerable and limiting the development of their gifts. Gilligan found that the girls who resisted conformity to a false image were girls who had a good relationship with a woman who was open and honest about her feelings and willing to be the person she was created to be.

Mothers and other women give adolescent girls a wonderful gift by spending time with them and developing friendships. Girls need to hear that we do not fit the "good girl" image but instead are in the process of becoming the women God wants us to be. Seeing in us authenticity and a willingness to stand for what we believe and do what we believe we are called to do will help girls resist the pressure to conform to the unreal standards others set for them. For girls passing through level II on their developmental journey, mature women companions are a great blessing.

Level III

Level III describes mature, adult forms of moral reasoning. Kohlberg found that people did not begin moving into level III until their midtwenties, at the earliest, and that maturity in moral development is not automatic with age. Many factors influence the age at which people begin using level III moral reasoning; some people may never develop those abilities.[49] For those concerned about the spiritual formation of children, it is important to know about level III moral reasoning, not because our children will be ready to move onto this level, but because, as we will see later, the progress of children along the moral development path is facilitated by walking with adults who are morally mature. Parents and teachers give a good gift to children when they continue to develop morally.

Source of Authority

As preadolescents, adolescents, and young adults live by the specific laws and expectations of level II, they grow in their understanding of the value and also of the limitations of the law. They come to realize that just laws are specific applications of moral principles. The moral principles that are behind the laws provide moral authority at level III. Most of the time stage 5 and stage 6 persons obey the laws and meet the expectations of others because in doing so they are acting on valued moral principles that are the bases for the laws and expectations. However, in some situations to apply one law violates another law. Those who are growing in their ability to put themselves in the other person's shoes may come to realize that some laws do not deliver justice to all people. To resolve injustice in the law or to decide how to act when laws conflict, level III moral reasoning turns to the principles behind the law.[50]

Defining Right and Wrong

Stage 5. Through interaction with a growing number of people, individuals discover that within a group or society there is a wide range of different values. They realize it is no more just for them to demand that others live by their values than that they be expected to abandon their values and live by another's. A way must be found to protect the life and the liberty of all members in the community or society. Group members must agree on basic values by which they all will live and on procedures for protecting the liberty of individuals to hold specific values, as long as they do not violate the legitimate liberty of others. At stage 5, right is upholding the rights and values upon which a society or a group has agreed. It is protecting the life of all people and guaranteeing them the liberty to live by their values.[51]

Stage 6. For the person using stage 6 moral reasoning, right is living by ethical principles that apply to all people. Principled judging and living requires that people understand moral principles and that they commit themselves to act on those principles in all situations. Kohlberg identified two justice principles that he believed guided the moral reasoning of stage 6. Those principles are equality of human rights and respect for the dignity of each individual.[52]

When a lawyer asked Jesus, "Which commandment in the law is the greatest?" Jesus responded by stating the principles from which all God's laws flow:

> "You shall love the Lord your God with all your heart, and with all your soul, and with all your mind." This is the greatest and first commandment.

And a second is like it: "You shall love your neighbor as yourself." On these two commandments hang all the law and the prophets.

Matthew 22:36–40

Jesus pointed the lawyer toward principled living.

Motivation to Do Right

Stage 5. Persons at stage 5 want to contribute to the welfare of others in the family, within friendships, at work, and in the community. This desire motivates them to invest time and energy in protecting the rights of others and in making the community or family a better place for everyone.[53] Mutual respect is important to persons at stage 5. They give respect and want to be respected by others in the community as reasonable, consistent individuals who are purposeful and who make a significant contribution. They respect themselves when they believe they are this kind of person. The desire for self-respect and community respect motivates stage 5 individuals to do what is right. They will avoid wrong to keep from losing respect.[54]

Stage 6. Persons using stage 6 moral reasoning are deeply committed to moral principles. To violate those principles would lead to self-condemnation.[55] The high value placed on moral principles and the desire to be a person of integrity motivates the stage 6 person to right attitudes and actions.

Awareness of Intentions

Stage 5. When judging an action, stage 5 moral reasoning takes into account motives and intentions, but good intentions do not make an act right at stage 5. If principles have been violated, the act is wrong, and the person must be held accountable for the action. Disapproval, however, may be expressed differently, depending on the intentions behind the action.[56]

Stage 6. For the stage 6 person, an act is right only if it applies the principle of love and respect for all persons.[57] Any action that violates those principles will grieve and at times stir anger within the principled person, even when the intentions that motivated the action were good. Stage 6 moral reasoning is not blind to intentions but holds persons accountable for their actions, while respecting their level of moral development. In situations where principled people intended to act in love and respect but the act had in fact violated those principles, they would not excuse the action but would acknowledge the failure and learn from it.

Taking the Perspective of Others

Stage 5. The growing ability to understand the perspective of individuals and groups quite different from themselves is one factor that causes people to develop stage 5 moral reasoning. Their ability to understand diverse perspectives causes them to see the need for procedures that can justly respond to the differences. They discover that without entering into formal agreements of commitment to one another, the needs of some are almost always ignored. This is particularly true of minorities, the young, and the poor.[58] To respect the perspectives of all, we need procedures for listening to one another and for finding ways to serve all. This is true in families as well as in churches, communities, nations, and international relations.

Stage 6. The principled moral judgment of stage 6 is not possible unless one can comprehend the perspective and needs of each person to be affected by a decision.[59] Ongoing moral development requires experience with an ever widening circle of persons. Only as we get to know people who are different from ourselves, and to know them well, can we put ourselves in their shoes. A person committed to principled living will invest time and energy getting to know the perspective of others.

The Value of Persons

Stage 5. Life is valued as a basic human right in stage 5 moral reasoning. No matter what their status in society, every person has a right to life. People are also valued and respected for their contribution to the welfare of the community.[60] There is an awareness that diversity enriches a community, which enhances appreciation for those who are different.

Stage 6. At stage 6, human life is valued regardless of contribution to society, and each person is treated with consideration and respect. Life is of greater value than any other consideration.[61] Stage 6 persons are often found investing their lives on behalf of the poor and the powerless.

Understanding Justice

Stage 5. At stage 5, justice is equity, which may require some inequality to adjust for differences. People at stage 5 realize a just decision cannot be reached if only one perspective is considered. The perspectives of all those involved in the situation must be heard and integrated if the decision is to be just. Justice also requires that laws be evaluated and changed if they are not guarding the rights and liberties of all, including minorities. In the area of corrective justice, stage 5 persons are not satisfied to simply punish offenders; they want penalties to contribute to change in the offender and in society.[62]

Stage 6. Justice, for stage 6 persons, is equal consideration for all who will bear the impact of the decision to be made. Special concern is held for the most disadvantaged—those whose voices are least likely to be heard or heeded. The justice principles that guide the reasoning of stage 6 individuals are positive statements of what one ought to do, not negative "thou shalt nots."[63] Living by principles is demanding; it requires that we go beyond avoiding specified actions and find ways to act on behalf of others that will make a positive difference in their lives.

FACILITATING MORAL DEVELOPMENT

Knowing how children reason morally helps us to understand their point of view and to be more accepting of them where they are on their developmental journey. But concerned parents and teachers want to be more than accepting; they want to make a positive contribution to the moral development of children. Is that possible? Do we know what is most likely to facilitate a child's moral development? Fortunately, the research findings of Piaget and Kohlberg do indicate how adults can most effectively encourage and support the moral development of children.

The four necessary causes of cognitive development identified by Piaget also stimulate moral development. Heredity and maturation govern the potential for development at any given point in a child's life. Trying to force development faster than the child is maturing is counterproductive. Understanding the pattern of moral development and the normal age range for development keeps us in step with the child and prevents the short-circuiting of moral development that occurs when adults try to force it prematurely or through the use of inappropriate means.

In addition to heredity and maturation, Kohlberg identified three other factors that provide the experience, social interaction, and process of equilibration necessary for moral development. These factors are role-taking (experience), participation in a just community (social interaction), and inner moral conflict or questioning (leading to the process of equilibration).[64] Parents and teachers can work with these factors for the good of children.

Role-Taking

The most important social experience for stimulating moral development is role-taking.[65] Role-taking involves putting oneself in the shoes of others; becoming aware of their thoughts, feelings, and attitudes; empathizing with them. We have seen that children begin life oblivious to the thoughts, feelings, and desires of others, locked in their egocentrism. What, then, causes the child to begin noticing what others are doing and wanting to imitate them or take their role? A sense of attachment, Kohlberg found, draws children into imitation and role-taking—a human attachment that requires the following characteristics:

1. Attachment involves similarity. [Humans become attached to other persons.]
2. Attachment involves love or altruism toward the other.
3. Attachment and altruism presuppose self-love.
4. Attachment involves a defined possessive bond or relation linking the self and the other.
5. Attachment presupposes the desire for esteem in the eyes of the other or for reciprocal attachment.[66]

When children feel attached to another, they want the other person to be pleased with them. Therefore, to try to discover what the other person wants, they watch, listen, and imitate him or her. As they imitate, they experience some of what the admired person experiences. This is role-taking.

Notice that children do not imitate just anyone. Love and a sense of belonging are essential components in attachment. We have the wonderful opportunity of influencing the children who love us and who sense a link with us; they watch and imitate the way we live. What a challenge! And there is more. Did you notice that self-love is also essential for attachment? By loving children, we help them feel loved and valued, making it possible for them to love themselves and others, to develop attachments, and to learn from those they love. Positive moral influence begins in a relationship of mutual love and belonging, which draws the child into imitation and role-taking.

Children first experience the joy of imitation in play.[67] With fascination, babies watch others clap their hands; then one day they reproduce the clapping. What fun! Preschoolers amuse us with what they choose to imitate. Several years ago my young niece and nephews played on the deck during a family vacation. "Hit it," they called. What were they doing? That morning they had watched their father and uncles water-skiing; now they were pretending to water-ski, ordering the driver of the imaginary boat to "hit it." Imitation brings pleasure and satisfaction to young children as they learn.

The ability to take the role of another grows as children participate in groups, and through those experiences they advance in moral development. Children have opportunities for role-taking as they participate first in their family, then in their peer group, and finally in other institutions such as the school and the church. But simple physical presence in a group is not enough to stimulate moral development; the group must provide certain crucial elements. One such element is emotional warmth. Families with morally mature children are characterized by emotional warmth.[68] Neither a harsh and punishing nor a totally permissive environment encourages moral development, but children flourish where loving respect flows between parents and children.

Morally healthy families value communication, trusting one another with their joys and their sorrows. Parents encourage children to share their opinions during family discussions and then take seriously those viewpoints, giving children the sense that they play a role in family decision making. When parents and children differ in their opinions, differences need to be discussed, with parents letting children express their perspectives and then parents further clarifying their position for the child. In this everyday decision making and discussion, children learn to take the role of others and to feel good about themselves as they share in the responsibility for the family.[69]

Kohlberg recommends what he calls *inductive discipline* as a way of facilitating moral development. In inductive discipline, parents help children become aware of the consequences of their actions, to discover the impact their actions have on others, and to take responsibility for those actions.[70]

As his mother and I attempted to visit, three-year-old David tried his best to gain our full attention. When the request that he play quietly went unheeded, David and Mommy left the room. A few minutes later David returned, leaned against me, and said, "I'm sorry, Aunt Cathy, for making it unhappy." David was being helped to realize the consequences of his actions and to take responsibility for them. He was growing in his ability to consider the needs of others—an essential skill for moral judgment.

When, within the family, children are given responsibilities, they experience new roles, exercise choice, discover the consequences of their actions for themselves as well as for others, and have opportunity to mature morally.[71] Responsibilities must, of course, match the maturity of the children and increase as they grow in ability to carry greater responsibility. Young children can begin to take responsibility for themselves and to exercise choice when parents let them select what they will wear. At first the choice could be between two appropriate options, extending eventually to full freedom to choose their clothing. When children begin school, the gift of an alarm clock can equip them for the responsibility of getting themselves ready for school on time.

When children carry responsibilities within the family that make a difference, they gain a sense of significance and discover how their actions have an impact on others. Parents can enhance feelings of significance by celebrating the contributions children make to the life of the family. When the dishwasher is loaded promptly, you can tell your child how good it made you feel to walk into a clean kitchen. Affirm the child who chose the activity for family night by commenting on how much fun it was. These are simple but meaningful celebrations.

Responsibilities must be real if children are to learn the consequences of actions. Too often parents short-circuit the learning potential of events by intervening so that the child does not have to bear the consequences that naturally flow from choices. When children plead for a pet, they often promise to feed it every day, but when the goldfish or the puppy goes without food, Mother steps in and takes over the responsibility. But if Sarah finds her goldfish floating dead in the bowl, she discovers that goldfish cannot survive if one forgets their promise to feed them. Mother can inform Tommy that she cannot let his new puppy go hungry, so he has a choice: He can feed the puppy as he promised, or the puppy will be given to someone who will feed it. Children need to discover the consequences of irresponsibility while the stakes are low rather than when their future or another human life is in their hands. In the process they discover that choices have consequences that can have an impact on others, and they will be better prepared to make moral choices.

It is important for children to know they have a role to play in creating the atmosphere of the home. One morning Teddy had apparently gotten up on the wrong side of the bed. Finally his mother said, "Take grumpy Teddy to his room and leave him there until nice Teddy can come out." To my surprise, four-year-old Teddy understood the order, went to his room, and came out later, ready to be a cheerful member of the family. He had space to be grumpy if he needed that, but he was also learning he had an important part to play in making his home a happy place. When children take this kind of responsibility for themselves and the family, their contribution needs to be celebrated. Of course, parents and teachers must not expect of their children what they are not willing to give themselves. Children are better able to contribute to community life when they can observe adults responding in responsible, considerate ways.

Moral development is enhanced when children are active participants in a setting where the discussion of viewpoints, values, and attitudes is encouraged, where the child's viewpoint is taken seriously, and the perspectives of adults and other children are also clearly shared. Kohlberg found that children growing up in homes characterized by such communication were the most advanced in their moral development. Children who interacted extensively with their peers were also more advanced than children who were socially isolated. Because children see one another as equals, mutual respect appears in their relationships with each other before they sense mutual respect with adults. Mutual respect makes it easier to see things from the other person's point of view and helps children take the roles of others. Role-taking among peers stimulates moral development. In the home, at school, and in other settings, children benefit from discussing reasons, communicating with one another, and participating in group decision making as part of their everyday experiences.[72]

Participation in a Just Community

Kohlberg believed that how one understands justice is at the heart of moral reasoning. Children must experience just treatment and participate in providing justice for others if they are to grow in their understanding of justice and to develop morally.[73] Children experience the home or classroom as just and fair when they are respected and when their viewpoint is asked for, listened to, and valued—when what they say makes a difference in the way things are done.[74] It is important that parents and teachers remember how children understand justice at each stage in their development and meet them where they are, while also giving them the opportunity to discover more adequate forms of justice.

Kohlberg found that mothers who used principled moral reasoning had children who were more morally mature than the children of mothers who were conventional in their moral judgments.[75] The principled mothers, with a more mature understanding of justice, may be able to give their children a home that is more just and in this way may facilitate their moral development.

Stimulating Moral Questions and New Understandings

What, you may ask, is the role of moral instruction in stimulating development? Is there no place for teaching children right and wrong? Yes, in addition to the experiences discussed so far in this chapter, words and new ideas are needed to guide and stimulate development.[76] However, adults engaged in the moral education of children face a major challenge. Children see the moral issues in a situation very differently from adults. Attempts at moral education are ineffective and even counterproductive unless the moral demands and instructions match the child's moral reasoning.[77]

Kohlberg found that children, as well as adolescents and adults, can comprehend moral reasoning that is one stage beyond the reasoning they currently use. When they hear moral messages two or more stages beyond them, they either fail to connect with the idea because it makes no sense to them, or they distort the message to fit their understanding and do not even hear the challenge to think in new ways. Children can understand moral instructions that use reasoning below their present stage, but they are not drawn to act on reasoning they have left behind as inadequate. Moral messages presenting concepts one stage higher stimulate development because children can understand them, and the concepts therefore challenge the limitations of their reasoning and introduce them to better ways of judging. When the adequacy of reasoning is questioned and new options are introduced, inner conflict and uneasiness builds. Children are attracted by reasoning one step beyond them to resolve the sense of inadequacy or conflict and to restore equilibrium.[78]

Effective moral education begins with parents and teachers listening, not talking. They must make a practice of listening to children to discover how they see events and to understand the reasoning they are using. With that understanding, we can meet children where they are and introduce them to better forms of moral judgment that are within their reach.[79]

Another challenge for parents and teachers is the difference in the ways children and adults perceive the morality of certain behaviors. Young children do not comprehend the moral issues in some behaviors that adults assume to be basic to the moral life. For example, we saw earlier that preschool children believe the worst lie is the one furthest from the truth. Being unaware of the importance of intentions, they are less troubled by the little lies that are told to protect themselves from punishment. Early elementary children, who believe right is whatever serves their own interests, do not see a moral problem in cheating if they have the opportunity to get a little help from a classmate's paper.

We do children a disservice when we force them to accept certain behaviors as "very bad" before they are able to understand the moral issue that makes the action bad. To force the issue prematurely teaches children not to think or not to try to understand right and wrong but just to accept the word of the authority and to comply without question. If children do not learn to think morally, they become adolescents who are at the mercy of whatever authority grasps their attention; when there is no authority to tell them what to do, they have no moral guidance.

The alternative is not to ignore cheating and lying but to approach the issues with awareness of the child's perceptions. First, lead children to look at their behavior and have them describe, in their own terms, what is good or bad. Encourage them to exercise their current moral reasoning in the situation. With an understanding of the child's view, the parent or teacher can introduce other considerations in terms that are within the child's comprehension, providing him or her with new ways to think about the issue.

Children need to know what moral behavior parents and teachers value. The reasons behind the values, however, must be expressed in ways that connect with the child's level of development. Understanding the characteristics of moral reasoning at the various stages of development prepares us to communicate with children. The rationale for some behavioral standards will be beyond the child's grasp. In those cases, parents or teachers need to make an administrative declaration, "This is the way we do it here," but must not present the behavior as a moral issue. Children should not be made to feel bad for not understanding or owning the moral value that makes the behavior right or wrong.[80]

Another way of raising new questions and stimulating moral development is to engage children in the discussion of moral dilemmas. They may be stories in which children face moral conflict or real situations in which children have experienced moral conflict. In such discussions, children should be helped to identify actions that could have been taken and the consequences that might flow from the actions. Ask not only *what* is the right thing to do, but *why* it would be right. The parent or teacher should give children opportunity to exercise their moral reasoning and also suggest questions to the children about issues their current moral judgments do not address. Children benefit by being in groups where they hear others discuss issues using moral reasoning a little more advanced than their own. The questions and more advanced ideas show up the limitations in their thinking and stimulate forward movement. These discussions are particularly influential when the persons involved are important to the child.[81]

The moral actions that surround children may also stimulate or inhibit moral development. Children need to see moral actions that demonstrate the moral concerns of stage 3—the unselfish care for others and the consideration of intentions or limitations. The actions rather than the words of morally principled mothers may explain why they tend to have children who are morally more mature than other children their age.[82] In moral actions, children may be able to see more mature moral concerns and responses before they can hear those concerns in verbal explanations. Observing moral actions that are guided by moral principles may enhance the child's readiness for moral development.

Although the cause and effect relationship between the moral actions of significant adults and the moral development of children is not fully understood, a relationship does exist. Adults who care about the moral development of children will want to be sure that their moral actions are consistent with their words. One of the best gifts we can give our children is that we be persons who continue to develop morally and persons of integrity whose words and actions are in harmony.

MORAL ACTIONS

So far we have been exploring how parents and teachers can facilitate the development of a child's moral reasoning. Although adults want children to make sound moral judgments, our concerns do not end with having equipped them to think well. We also want them to act morally.

What influences whether moral judgments become moral actions? Through experiments to test the honesty of children, Kohlberg found that moral action is influenced by the child's level of moral reasoning and ego strength. *Ego strength* refers to a set of inner functions that include the intellectual ability to understand a situation well enough to predict the consequences of actions, the tendency to choose the long-term greater good over short-term immediate rewards, and the ability to focus attention on a task for a significant period of time. Other researchers have also found that children who act morally and resist delinquent behavior are characterized by these factors of ego strength that would be commonly identified as a strong will.[83]

In Kohlberg's experiments, the children most likely to cheat were children who used level I moral reasoning and were high in ego strength, and the children who used level II moral reasoning and had low ego strength or willpower. The strong-willed level I children had the ability to assess the situation and decide they could probably cheat and get away with it. Their moral understanding valued what would give them the greatest reward and provided them with no reason not to cheat. Therefore, they took the risk and did what they wanted to do. Level II moral reasoning usually leads children to believe cheating is wrong. They are taught that good people do not cheat, and they know the laws of home and school say they must not cheat. Ego strength equips children to assess the situation and to see the value of not cheating, and it provides the willpower to resist the temptation of immediate gratification and to choose to do what they believe is right. Without ego strength, children do not have the power to resist short-term rewards and do what they know is right.[84]

Strong-willed children are a challenge for parents and teachers who often wish that they would be more compliant. However, that strong will can be a power for good when teamed with maturing moral reasoning.

Kohlberg's description of ego strength provides insight into ways in which adults might help children strengthen their will. Through inductive discipline and discussions of moral dilemmas, we can assist children to grow in their ability to assess situations and to predict the consequences of actions. Helping children to focus their attention and to increase their attention span strengthens their ability to resist temptation. Attentive children focus in on instructions given and the task before them. When their attention is grasped by constructive activity, they are not tempted by inappropriate behavior.[85]

Parents can help their children focus attention when, for example, they give toddlers a manageable number of toys with which to play. Children enjoy playing longer with one toy when they are not distracted by too many options. Some parents regularly store some toys and bring out others to keep the play environment interesting but not distracting.

Time spent looking at picture books with toddlers and reading to older children makes focused attending a pleasant experience for them. Or adults who enjoy nature and take the time to look for beautiful leaves, rocks, or shells can draw children into the focused enjoyment of God's creation. And to think that these enjoyable times together can strengthen a child's ability to resist temptation!

Teachers who design interesting learning activities help children learn to focus their attention. Some children struggle with attention deficit disorders and will find it difficult to keep focused because their attention is easily distracted. Adults who care about these children will see that they get the help needed to manage the disorder.

Children can also be helped to strengthen their will as they learn they will not always get what they want when they want it. As noted earlier, *will* is the ability to resist a strong desire for a short-lived reward and to respond to a presently weaker desire for a greater long-term good. It depends on remembering other experiences in which waiting and doing the right thing was the best choice.[86] Children need to experience the satisfaction of enjoying something they have waited for.

Sarah and her father sat on a hilltop by the lake, eating a picnic supper together. Sarah had waited for this special time of having Daddy all to herself. She had accepted the need for him to be away on business trips and had let Jonathan, her brother, have an evening out with Dad, knowing that her turn would come. She could then experience the pleasure of what she had waited for—the satisfaction of delayed gratification.

An allowance of money and the freedom to choose how to spend it can teach children the value of delayed gratification. If children buy the first things they see, their money may be gone when they find what they really want. Next time, they would be more inclined to wait and be sure that they know what they want before spending their money. However, this lesson will not be learned if parents always give out money on demand when the allowance is gone. Through experience children need to learn the reality that they will be deprived of many greater rewards if they choose to take lesser rewards along the way.

FAITH AND THE MORAL LIFE OF CHILDREN

As we consider the moral reasoning and actions of children, it is important to examine the relationship between religion and morality. Religion and morality are closely intertwined for Christians and Jews because their God is deeply concerned about love and justice, calling people to act morally. They believe God is the source of the strength needed to do what is right.

Moral reasoning makes it possible for people to decide what actions would be just and moral in a given situation, but moral reasoning does not tell why one should do what is moral when it will not result in personal advantage. Faith in a just and loving God gives a meaningful purpose for accepting one's duty and being moral.[87] As children meet Jesus and are introduced to God at work in Bible stories, they see love and justice in action. A growing love for Jesus causes them to want to please him and to be like him. This gives them a reason to be moral. Children also need the comfort of knowing they can ask God for the strength to do what is right, even when it is hard.

Accepting moral responsibility is an essential link between deciding what ought to be done and doing it. When faced with a moral conflict, there are several steps between awareness and action. We first interpret the situation using the level of moral reasoning of which we are capable, and then we decide what the right action should be. Knowing what ought to be done, we next consider whether we have an obligation to act—to be moral. A commitment to be like Jesus and to do what he would want us to do gives us a reason to accept moral responsibility. Finally, the ego strength discussed earlier turns the knowledge of what is right and the acceptance of responsibility into moral action.[88] Children as well as adults who truly want to live for Jesus have a compelling reason to be moral.

Kohlberg did not intend to give a plan for Christian education or the spiritual formation of children. However, many of his findings provide Christian parents and teachers with significant insights into how they can work with children, facilitating their moral and spiritual formation.

Robert Coles is another student of children and their moral life. For more than two decades he has listened to children talk about their lives—children from several countries, the very poor and the rich. Many of the children with whom he worked found themselves surrounded by social upheaval or poverty that threatened their continued existence.

Ruby was one of the children with whom Coles worked in the 1960s. Each morning and each afternoon for months, six-year-old Ruby Bridges, an African-American child, walked through a mob of adults who yelled threats at her. This was the price she paid to attend school—a school that had been all white until she enrolled.

Coles's method was to spend many hours over several years getting to know children in depth.[89] Out of these encounters, he developed a profound respect for the moral courage and insight of children—particularly those who lived with tragedy and pain. How could six-year-old Ruby face her assailants each morning with a smile and pray for them every night? What Coles saw and heard caused him to question the adequacy of psychoanalytic and developmental theories to explain the moral life of children. As he read Piaget and Kohlberg, whom he respected, he kept remembering the moral behavior of some children whose actions seemed to be much beyond what the developmentalists believed possible in childhood. Coles felt understanding the moral life of children called for more than measuring abstract moral thinking in a research setting through listening to children respond to predesigned moral dilemmas.[90]

Coles went to the children and, in their familiar setting, listened to them talk about and reflect on their real-life encounters and actions. In *The Moral Life of Children* he tells the stories of some of the children with whom he worked and reflects on their lives. He does not lay out a theory of moral formation or empowering. Instead, he asks what could explain a child's moral strength and then identifies some factors that may have contributed to it. Marty and Eduardo demonstrated the moral strength Coles describes. Marty's life was hard. As the child of migrant workers, she had known nothing but poverty. Her father's death in an accident caused by a drunk driver added grief to her young life. Eduardo, a desperately poor ten-year-old Brazilian boy, worked hard to help support his family. Although criminal activities could bring fast money, he chose to avoid such means for survival. In the lives of Marty and Eduardo, Coles saw the following characteristics: compassionate regard for others, stubborn persistence, modesty and candor about personal failings, moral pride or self-respect, moral purpose or a reason to act morally.[91] What caused these characteristics to form in Marty and Eduardo? What gave Ruby the strength to integrate a school? Coles does not answer these questions, but he notes that religion and faith played an important role in each child's life.

When wondering about Ruby's moral courage, Coles states, "If I had to offer an explanation, though, I think I would start with the religious tradition of black people."[92] Children were taught that God had a purpose for them, and those who grasped that message had a reason to be strong. The preaching at church also told Ruby the road to heaven would not be easy. The hard experiences of life, therefore, did not take her by surprise. Ruby believed what the preacher said, and his words supplied her with direction and strength.[93]

The children with whom Coles worked developed their morality through intense experience. Of Eduardo, Coles writes, "He has learned after only ten years on earth to stay alive, to master a modern city, to spar with death, even anticipate its arrival, contemplate its many possibilities: a grown mind's moral imagination at work in the continuing life of one of this earth's vulnerable children."[94] In years, Eduardo was a child, in experience an adult.

Through the hard experiences of life, Eduardo became morally mature. But Coles freely acknowledges that those who become morally strong are surrounded by many who are destroyed by similar circumstances. He leaves us with the sense that there is mystery involved. We do not have all the answers. We do not fully understand how one becomes morally mature and strong.

Coles cautions us against a narrow, simplistic understanding of the moral life. We can be guided by insights from Erikson, Piaget, and Kohlberg on ways in which parents and teachers can facilitate the development of children. However, we must never assume that we control the process. There is mystery in each child's becoming and in each child's marvelous potential that is strengthened in a vital faith community.

Six

KNOWING GOD
IN CHILDHOOD

E arly in my childhood," says Walter Wangerin, "I suffered a spiritual crisis. I can't remember *how* early this was, but I was young enough to crawl beneath the church pews, small enough to be hauled back up by my mother one-handed, yet old enough to wish to see Jesus. I wanted to see Jesus with my own eyes."[1]

When do children begin to think about God? How do they come to know God? What have we learned about the faith of children and how it forms? Does it really make any lasting difference what image a small child has of God? These are important questions to explore.

THE YOUNG CHILD'S IMAGE OF GOD

From Piaget's findings on cognitive development, some religious educators concluded that children are not ready to really understand God and faith because they are not capable of abstract thought, which is not expected to develop until adolescence.[2] When the focus of attention for religious education is on the cognitive knowing of God, adults overlook the young child's experience of God. Children's comments and questions about God are viewed as cute but distorted or simply as the repetition of what they have heard adults say, and unimportant in the long run. Adolescence is assumed by many to be the period of life in which young people come to know God—the time for serious instruction in the faith.

Adults who listen to children attentively and know them well are uncomfortable with such assumptions. They believe children are sensitive and responsive to God. Evidences of profound spiritual experience in early childhood come from many sources. Sofia Cavalletti, in her book, *The Religious Potential of the Child*, reports examples of children who had no religious training but who expressed a deep, joy-inspiring belief in the Creator God.[3] Alister Hardy, a British researcher, "invited those who 'felt that their lives had in any way been affected by some power beyond themselves' to write an account of the experience and the effect it had on their lives." Of the four thousand accounts received, 15 percent were reports from childhood. The events could be described in detail thirty or fifty years later; they had been profound experiences.[4] Ana-Maria Rizzuto believes that children first become conscious of God between two and three years of age. Childhood images of God, she asserts, are powerful and influence us throughout a lifetime.[5]

How does this early God consciousness dawn? How do children construct their picture of God? Children blend together several elements as they form their image of God.

Looking for the Cause

Around the age of three, children begin to bubble over with questions about causes. As infants they discover sensorimotor cause and effect. When they pull a blanket, the toy lying on it comes closer. By the age of three their cognitive development makes it possible to wonder what causes the phenomenon they see in the world around them. Based on their experience, children assume everything is caused by someone acting on it. Who makes the clouds move? Who makes the grass grow? Who makes the leaves move? Who made the wind? They want to know. The questions seem endless, with each answer stimulating another question.

Young children do not seem to find scientific answers satisfying. They keep pushing for the ultimate cause of what they see happening in nature—the prime mover—until parents, time after time, give the answer, "God" (or for those who do not believe in God, a supreme force or being). This intense questioning occurs at a time when children have an idealized view of parents. They think Mommy and Daddy can do anything, and then they discover someone or something greater than their parents—God. In this first conscious awareness of God, children are greatly impressed with God's power and perfection.[6]

Relating to Parents and Significant Adults

Children form their image of God in the context of relating to their parents and other significant adults. God is an all-powerful, all-knowing parent who tends to take on the characteristics of parents, as the child perceives them. Children mix together in their understanding of God both facts and fantasies about their parents.[7] For example, children who experience faithful care and are reassured of love even when disciplined are likely to have an image of a God who loves them dearly and consistently. Their God reflects the fact of their experience with parents. A child whose mother suddenly becomes ill and is hospitalized, however, may imagine that mother went away to punish the child for being naughty. That imagined cause of the mother's absence may lead the child to believe that God abandons those who are not perfect. The image of God may also include what a child wishes the parents were like, or the fear of a parent may carry over into a fear of God.[8]

Some children in abusive situations develop an image of God as the idealized parent, and their God brings them great comfort. Barb grew up feeling rejected by her parents. As a young child, she would escape the psychological abuse by going to her room and imagining that her daddy was a king. In her fantasies they would talk and do fun things together, and she would sit on her daddy king's lap as he held and loved her. Years later as she worked through the long-term effects of the abuse, in anger Barb cried out to God, "Where were you when that little girl needed you?" The answer came back, "I was your daddy king," and that brought healing comfort to her. But not all abused children seem able to imagine a loving God; instead, many fear God as they fear their parents.

Children sometimes imagine and fear harsh punishment that has no basis in the facts of their experience with their parents. When they do something wrong, the active imaginations of these children create a feared punishment blown completely out of proportion to their parents' disciplining practices. In an earlier chapter, we saw that young children believe in imminent justice, that they will certainly be punished for wrongdoing, and that punishment is fair. Some such children fear God, because God is seen as the one who will punish them when adults do not know about their sin. As we will discuss more fully later, it is important to listen to children and to know what they are building into their image of God. Caring adults want to help children discover and drop destructive distortions in their understanding of God.

From the very early days of life, children acquire critical pieces to build into their image of God. They are born to parents who were formed in families and who developed their own images of God when they were very young. Consciously and unconsciously, parents communicate their images of God to their children.

For example, parents hold some view of their child's conception. They may see the new life as a gift from God, the result of love, an unwanted accident, or a punishment for sexual sin. Through the stories parents tell about the birth and through their unconscious attitudes, comments, and behavior, children form a perception of whether their birth was a positive or a negative act of God or simply a biological accident. These perceptions give children a sense of worth and meaning.[9] Such influences exist in the environment of all children.

Who we are as adults, what we believe about God, and how we think and feel permeate the world in which our children live and grow. We cannot shield them from that. In relationship with us they discover themselves and construct their God, whose valuing of them looks like the sense of worth they see reflected from us.

Another factor at work in the early weeks of life is what some call *mirroring*.[10] Babies spend many hours in the arms of their mother and father, or other significant adults, comfortably being fed and looking into their eyes. What babies see in the eyes of their parents and others is very important. They see what the parent (or adult) sees. They see themselves as they are seen by the parent, and in that reflection they gain the first picture of themselves. If the eyes of the mother or father reflect deep love and pleasure in the baby, he or she sees the self as lovable and pleasing. If the eyes are unresponsive, the baby does not see the self and feels ignored, rejected. That experience launches the child on a journey of striving to be noticed, to earn approval. Rizzuto believes that in creating their earliest representations of God, children transfer what they have seen in the eyes of their mothers, and other significant adults, and see that image of themselves in the eyes of God.

Rizzuto also describes the powerful influence of the infant's dedication, baptism, or circumcision. Most parents, even those who do not practice religion, want to present their child to God through a religious ritual. Before children have any self-awareness, many are given to God or marked for God. From their earliest days, being God's child is woven into the unfolding story of the child's identity.[11]

How seriously do we take infant baptism or dedication? Do we usually think of it solely as a parental act, which hopefully directs the parents as they guide their child through life? Or do we see the child being marked for God—intentionally given to God for the mysterious working of God's grace through all of life, beginning in infancy? We can enhance the role of infant baptism or dedication by making this event special. We can encourage parents to take pictures that portray each feature of the day and to keep a memento, possibly the clothes the baby wore when being given to God. Over the years, parents can look at the pictures with the child, handle the little dress or suit, and tell the story of that special day—the day they gave him or her to God to be God's special child. Also, trust God to be at work within the child's life.

Yes, our children must one day make the faith their own and give themselves to God, but God graciously draws them toward that day. Although God respects our freedom of choice and our children may reject grace, I believe their choice is influenced toward God when we give them to God, trust them to grace, and open ourselves to reflect God's love.

Symbolizing Comfort and Constancy

At the core of Rizzuto's understanding of "the birth of the living God" is the concept of transitional object representation. An object representation is the ability to recall through memory the perception of an object as the person experienced it earlier. These perceptions are stored in our memory banks, but not just as static snapshots of the objects or events. The memories include a complex mix of facts, imagined meanings, feelings, sights, smells, and sounds. Even very young infants store the memory of visceral sensations such as the comfort of being held, caressed, and fed. As soon as babies discover that the ball or the rattle still exists when they cannot see it, when they develop object constancy, they begin storing their memories of things—object representations. Memories of an object or an event may be called into consciousness at any time by a thought, fantasy, feeling, sight, smell, or sound connected to the memory.[12]

But what, you may ask, is a *transitional* object representation? In her writing, Rizzuto often mentions *transitional space*. This is the place where the adult's imagination and creative processes work, where we play around with our perceptions of material, relational, and spiritual reality to discover meaning, and where we envision new ways of responding in the future. For young children, this is where they play—where through fantasy and imagination they act out relationships and learn to cope with their real world. In this world of imagination, children create a "colorful crowd of characters" such as imaginary playmates and monsters. They also create their image of God.[13]

When toddlers begin to walk and to enjoy increasing autonomy, they still suffer from the fear of separation from their parents. They need something to give comfort when parents are absent. Their imagination creates for them what Rizzuto calls a transitional object. It is an object that symbolizes the relationship with parents, which has the feeling of the parents' presence connected to it. Children who carry their blanket with them carry the comfort of the parents' love in the blanket. Hugging the special teddy bear in the dark assures the child of the consistency and love of the mother and father.[14] God may be such a transitional object for children who attach to God feelings of security and love; imagining God present with them can then be a great comfort. We must not forget, however, that if children have attached negative feelings to God, thoughts of God can bring terror and dread.[15]

Discovering the Difference

The unseen creations of the child's mind are very real, and therefore, young children believe easily in the reality of a God who cannot be seen. Although God is believed in, along with imaginary play-mates, fairies, and monsters, God is very different from their other imaginings. Adults believe in God, and children know they do not believe in the other creations of a child's imagination.

Children hear adults talk about God in respectful tones. They hear God's name in many places, whether in profanity, in the flow of con-versation, or in a "God bless you" after a sneeze. At church children see their parents and many other adults singing and talking to God, bowing in worship, and responding to God. In classes at church, adults lead the children in singing songs about God, in talking to God through prayer, and in telling them stories about God. Even parents who do not believe in God must explain to their children that they are different from others who the children see attending churches and who believe in the God they worship there. The way in which adults speak about God gives the unseen God a reality for children that their other imagined persons do not have.[16] We need not fear that children with creative imaginations will make God into nothing more than their other fantasies. The unseen God is real to children.

The Redefining Process

Young children think deeply about God and, just as they want to know more about their parents and how they do things, they also want to know more about God. Their questions come out of their own expe-riences: Where does God sleep? Does God like vegetables? How does God go to the bathroom? Unfortunately, adults often ignore these seemingly silly questions and fail to give children answers. Such responses leave children on their own to create answers for themselves. Although the child's image of God is always a combination of concrete elements found in life and of elements provided by the child's creativ-ity, ignoring their questions deprives children of the concrete under-standings we could offer and leaves them with some imaginary pieces that could have been replaced with better, more assuring images.[17]

Once the child's image of God has formed, and we have seen that it forms very early in life, it cannot be forced out of existence. It can be pushed down and repressed, thrown aside as an irrelevant toy from an earlier age, used as it is, or refined and transformed, but the image of God has a continuing life. Children face a struggle when parents tell them not to believe in God; they must find some way of reconciling what parents say with the image that has already formed within themselves. Some children continue to believe in secret. One of Rizzuto's patients, the daughter of militant atheists, remembered locking herself in her bedroom at the age of seven, kneeling on the floor for a long time, and praying, "Please let there be a God." Knowing that she was disobeying her parents, the little girl felt guilt and fear, but her need to worship was so great that she did what was prohibited—she prayed.[18] How amazing to realize hunger for God can be so intense in young children.

We do not give children their primary understanding of God through formal religious instruction. Even young children come to church with their own God. Our teaching is secondary to the primary image they have formed. In formal education, children are introduced to new ideas about God and must reconcile their image of God with what the teacher tells them about God. As we teach children, at home and in the church, we do not give them our understanding of God; rather, we guide them as they reshape their God in the light of what they learn from us and in their ever expanding life experiences.[19]

At any point in life our understanding of God is influenced by our experiences, the point of development reached in our cognitive capacities, and our sense of self and of others. Preschoolers normally have a concrete, anthropomorphic, imaginative image of God, which may serve them very well. But if God is not to be thrown away as a worn-out teddy bear, that early image of God must be reshaped and transformed. In each stage of development the image of God must grow and be redefined, using new capacities of reasoning and relating so that the current understanding of God is adequate for the challenges of the new stage in life.[20] It is impossible to give persons an image of God in childhood that will be adequate for a lifetime. The primary image of God is powerful and lasting, but the relationship with God must continually be transformed. Coming to know God is a lifelong process.

Much of the secondary, formal religious education offered to children focuses on learning about God and influences the shape of their conscious understanding of God and religion.[21] The primary image of God formed by the child early in life tends to work at the subconscious level. If the primary image is not redefined, it may cause a person to have one God in the mind and another in the depths of the heart.

When the God of the primary image is loving and gracious, it may lead a child, teenager, or adult to be uncomfortable with and finally to reject the secondary image of a harsh, demanding God given to them through teaching and preaching. On the other hand, some adults cannot trust God to be gracious and forgiving. They may have been well taught and may clearly understand with their minds the gracious characteristics of God. But if their primary image of God is as a parent who punished for wrong but never expressed forgiveness or one who was distant and not there for them, at the deep core of their being the negative view of God will rule and their heart will not be able to grasp what their head knows. The child's image of God is not to be ignored.

As you live and work with children, listen for fearful, destructive distortions in their view of God. Do children express fear or focus on punishment when they talk about God? Assure them of God's love through your love and stories of God's love and by rejoicing with them over evidences of God's love. Through drawing, children can express concepts they cannot verbalize. Researchers working with children often ask them to draw a picture of God and then have them tell about it. This is an approach parents and teachers can also use to gain a better understanding of a child's God.

Adults assist children in the refining and reshaping of their image of God by responding to the children's questions—even the ones that seem unimportant to us. Questions indicate an active mind, a teachable moment, and a desire for us to talk with them about God. When the three-year-old child asks, "Where does God sleep?" we have the privilege of responding, "Guess what? God never sleeps. God is different from us and is always watching over us. Isn't that wonderful?"

It is important to answer the question being asked and not to give an answer bigger than the question, an answer for which the child is not yet ready. As mentioned earlier, sometimes the appropriate answer to a child's question is, "What do you think?" The child's response often helps us discover what he or she really wants to know. If we let the questions of children guide us step-by-step in telling them about God, the questions will cease when they are satisfied with our answers and will begin again when they are ready for more.

Never give a child an answer of which you are not sure. If the child raises a question with which you are still struggling, be honest. "That's a hard question," you can say. "I'm still trying to understand that too."

You can then share some possible answers or the piece of the answer that you do believe.[22]

Saturday afternoon as I worked on the story of the Exodus for children's worship the next morning, I suddenly panicked. "Finally," the story read, "the firstborn of all the Egyptian families and animals died. But not the people of God. They were safe. Death passed over them (Exodus 12:21–30)."[23] I feared that Jonathan might be in children's worship for that story. A year earlier Jonathan's fifteen-year-old sister, the firstborn in their family, had died of cancer. What would I say if Jonathan asked, "Why was Angela not safe?" My first response was to skip the story, but Jonathan would have to face that question someday. What if the question was already in his mind unformed and painful, with no answer? Finally I decided to tell the story, and if the hard question came I would have to say, "Jonathan, I don't understand why God protected some people and not others. I'm still trying to answer that question. But one thing I do know, God loves Angela, and she is very happy now and free from pain. And I also know that God loves you and cares very much when you miss Angela and hurt inside."

In times of crisis, children need answers to their questions—even those they do not know how to ask. Parents or adult friends can help them express those questions. When Donna returned from the hospital after the death of her newborn, she noticed a distinct change in the behavior of her six-year-old daughter. Towanna had always been a helpful, cooperative child, but now she disobeyed and refused to cooperate. "Towanna," Donna asked, "are you angry at God for taking our baby?" The wise mother's query unleashed a flood of questions and angry feelings from the little girl. Together they talked about their sorrow and reaffirmed God's love for them and for their baby. By being sensitive and responsive to the questions of children, we can help them refine and shape their image of God in times when they are vulnerable to distortions that could cut them off from sensing God's comforting love.

God's Part

Some of you may be experiencing discomfort as you read this chapter. Throughout this chapter we have discussed the *child's* image of God. But where is God in all this, you may be asking.

Since the tendency to create an image of God seems to exist within young children whether or not they have religious influences in their home, I would say that this tendency is a creation gift from the Creator God. Genesis 1:27 states, "So God created humankind in his image, in the image of God he created them; male and female he created them." Human beings were created in the image of God. We arrive with no awareness of ourselves but with the need, over time, to differentiate and to know ourselves. That process begins in the first months of life.

If we truly are created in God's image, we must know God in order to fully know ourselves and who we can be. God has equipped human beings to begin that quest very early, and God's intention was that from birth the faithful, loving care of parents would provide experiences out of which the child could construct a clear, health-giving image of God. Even in our fallen world where God's good plan is marred, God can graciously work in the natural processes of living to draw the child toward an unfolding understanding and experience of God.

Many years ago Augustine said, "Thou [speaking of God] hast created us for thyself and our hearts are restless until they are found in thee." Even young children experience that restless desire, which leads them to want to know God. Constructing their image of God is their response to the pull of God, the beginning of getting to know God.

Adults in Partnership with Children

God chooses to work not only within individual children but through the families and faith communities in which they live and grow. We give our children a precious gift when we experience a growing relationship with God. When we are growing spiritually, God is real to us and we feel excitement and love for God, which leads to worship. As children sense that reality, love, and worship in the lives of adults around them, their image of God is confirmed and enhanced.

Many parents want to be the kind of persons their children need them to be, but they do not know how. God is faithful to guide us in our spiritual growth as we respond and let the Holy Spirit teach and lead us. One way the church can assist is to provide a structure of small groups that bring people together to support one another in their spiritual growth. These may be groups of couples whose children are of similar ages, separate groups for young mothers and for young fathers, or groups like extended families that are made up of older and younger couples along with single persons. Whatever the makeup of the group, the purpose is for the maturing of each person's faith and for giving support to one another for living the faith in every area of life. Groups can study the Scripture, share their joys and sorrows, successes and failures, and pray for one another.

Spiritual growth may also be stimulated through a relationship with a mentor—an older person who becomes a spiritual friend to a younger person. In response to the younger person's questions about being a godly man or woman in the home, community, and workplace, the mentor can share wisdom gleaned from living and walking with God. The church serves its people well when it encourages them to seek a mentor, prepares more mature members to be mentors, and provides the means whereby those wanting a mentor and those willing to be a mentor are brought together.

Parents and those who work with children need to look at their image of God. How do I really see God? is an important question on which to reflect personally, in a small group, or with a mentor. Since our image of God has an impact on the living of our Christian life and we communicate that image to our children, we want to be sure that our image truly reflects God. Those who discover great disparity between their knowledge of God and their inner picture of God need to seek the help of a pastor or a counselor to uncover the root of the negative image of God and to reshape that image. This may call for the healing of painful memories, but, if the person is willing to work through the pain, it will bring a great release. As adults, who we are and how we see God are important to the spiritual formation of our children.

If accepting this responsibility induces stress and perfectionistic striving, our efforts may be counterproductive. Polly Berrien Berends, in her book *Gently Lead: How to Teach Your Children about God While Finding Out for Yourself*, offers helpful insights out of her experience as a Christian mother.

> The best things your children will learn about God will be from watching you try to find out for yourself. Jesus said, "Seek and ye shall find." They will not always do what you tell them to do, but they will be—good and

bad—as they see you being. If your children see you seeking they will seek—the finding part is up to God.[24]

• To be a good parent or a good Sunday school teacher of children, we do not need to be people who have arrived; God simply calls us to be on the way, seeking, finding, and rejoicing in what we find. As we regularly and naturally read the Bible to find God's wisdom for our lives, talk to God about everyday events, and take a moment to listen for God's responding idea, and as we regularly worship God with others, our children will observe and come to value these activities also. God becomes increasingly real to children as they have opportunity to participate with us in the living of our faith and in the worship of God spontaneously in the flow of everyday life and in the gatherings of the faith community.

THE SEARCHING OF OLDER CHILDREN

Rizzuto provides us with an understanding of young children and their fascination with God. But as children begin to distinguish between fantasy and reality, do most of them leave God behind? As their lives expand and they develop an interest in science and technology, do they lose interest in this unseen God? Robert Coles would answer with a resounding no.

Coles is a child psychiatrist and anthropologist who has worked with children in many countries of the world. As he talked with children and listened to them give their thoughts on many different subjects, the frequency with which the children mentioned God and religious ideas greatly impressed him.[25] Finally Coles decided to explore the spiritual life of children. He focused the study on eight- to twelve-year-old children and interviewed over five hundred of them from several different countries.[26]

Coles's interviews involved many hours of conversation with the children on their home turf. He listened intently and discovered that in relaxed conversation with an adult who has become a friend, children express thoughts and insights that seldom show up in formal interviews or on tests. Coles came to see children as young seekers, asking the deep questions of life more often and more intensely than most adults realize. Older children try to make sense out of their lives; they want to understand what is happening and why. In that process they often turn to spiritual resources. They think "long and hard about who God is, about what God might be like." In quiet times alone their thoughts turn toward God, and this is true even for children whose families are not religious.[27]

When children talk about God and what they think on the deep questions and challenges of their lives, statements from parents, coaches, pastors, and teachers are woven into their understandings and answers. However, many children think deeply on their own about the insights they have learned from others and integrate them with their own wondering and conclusions. They seek and construct important understandings to guide their living, and their thinking is not a carbon copy of the adults around them. Their understandings deserve respect.

Biblical stories play an important role in the elementary child's search for answers. Coles found that children relate the experiences of biblical characters to the events of their own lives. As children think about these stories, they see themselves in the characters and see God working and relating to those biblical people. Certain stories grab children, inspire their imagination, and draw them to reflect on life, meaning, and God.[28]

As Coles talked with Christian children, he was impressed by how important Jesus was to them. He had the sense that in a special way they saw Jesus as a children's Savior. Children identified with him because he had been a child, just as they were. His life had a purpose, and that interested children who wonder about their future. Children frequently talked to Coles about Jesus' "visit"—as they called it—to earth and contemplated the reason for his coming. Repeatedly they expressed fascination with the miracles of Jesus. They were attracted to a Jesus who can heal the sick and raise the dead.[29]

For many children Jesus was far more than a historical figure. They thought a lot about him, talked to him in prayer, and wondered what it will be like to meet him someday. Mary, one of the children interviewed by Coles, gives us a glimpse of one child's thoughts about and relationship with Jesus.

When I pray to Him, I thank Him for coming here, and I tell Him I look forward a lot to seeing Him. . . . When I get to. . . . I wonder what He'll say to us! . . . I think He'll smile, though. My mom says you should think of Jesus as your best friend. . . . He's not like us, . . . He's God. . . . He probably doesn't eat and sleep. . . . He might not need a chair. Does He breathe? It's hard to know.[30]

Using what she knows about Jesus, Mary relates to him as a friend while she continually searches for more understanding, all with the concrete perspective of a child.

When children need help to be good or with their personal problems, they often turn to Jesus to guide them, because he was once a child and understands. One child told Coles that when he did not feel good and did not want to talk to anyone else, he would think of Jesus and talk to him. The child did not consider these times as prayer; he was just talking to Jesus, his friend. And the child had the sense that Jesus talked back: "Sometimes I'll say something, and I talk back to myself, and it's me talking back but it sounds better than me; I mean smarter. It could be Jesus saying something to me using my own voice."[31] Jesus can be very real to older children.

Reference to God's voice was a repeating theme Coles heard while talking with children; they believed God spoke to them. Children understand the thoughts that come to them while talking with God to be God's voice. A Jewish boy stated, "No one talks to me the way God does—He gets me thinking, and then I hear Him. . . . He doesn't speak to us when we pray; we speak to ourselves. But it's Him telling us what to say—to tell ourselves."[32]

Margarita was a very poor Brazilian child whose mother was ill. As Margarita thought of the future she and her brothers and sisters faced if their mother died, fear gripped her heart. When she compared her poverty to the abundance of the rich, anger overflowed at the injustice. When she was most upset she would talk to Jesus. "He is all I have," she said. Margarita told Coles,

When I leave [the shack where she lived] to go on a walk and tell Him what's on my mind, He doesn't give me the time of day. If I shout, He shuts up. If I tell Him how much I love Him, He won't blink—no sounds. But if I'm really in low spirits and not thinking of Him—thinking of myself and worrying what will happen to us, what will happen *next* to us—it's then that He takes me by surprise, completely. I hear Him and He'll say, "Margarita, you are looking too far ahead. First, try to get to the evening, the sunset; then try to get to the morning, the sunrise." When I hear Him, I feel calmer.[33]

Reflecting on his time of learning from Margarita, Coles said:

Her interest in God, I realized much later, was far more important than I allowed myself to notice at the time. The listening she did to God turned out to be the mainstay of her life. His voice uplifted her spirits when nothing else could. To her, His voice was . . . not that of anyone she knew, certainly not the priest's; and yet I gradually discovered a certain resemblance between the thrust of his comments, his homilies, and what she heard God say in His moments of expressed concern for her.[34]

Hearing God's voice is very real and important in the experience of many children. As Coles listened to children talk about God's voice, he did hear the voices of parents and other adults who were significant to the child, but there was more. For the children, hearing God's voice was more than simply remembering what they had been taught. What they had been taught was a significant piece of their relationship with God, but the words that came to them from God had a special way of calming their fears and directing their actions.

Not only do children hear God's voice, many also see God's face. Picturing God's face is a means Christian children all over the world use to connect with God, Coles found. "When I woke up and was scared," one child reported, "I pictured His face: the big eyes and a smile. *He* wasn't scared, so I decided I shouldn't be either." Another child pictured God's face when he was doing his best. "When I'm running and I see His smile, I feel my body change—it's like shifting into high gear, my daddy says."[35]

Coles often asked children to draw a picture of God. Of the 293 drawings he received, 87 percent pictured the face of God.[36] When children imagine what God is like, it seems that they see God's face. Coles found that for many Christian children, drawing God's face helped them to focus on God concretely and to know what they believed about God. Often children understand more about God than they have words and logic to express. Children can often talk about a picture they have drawn with words they could not put together before drawing the picture.[37]

Elementary and middle school children have not arrived in their understanding of God, and they know it. As they talk about God, many unanswered questions are mixed in with what they believe and experience of God. They accept that mix of the known and the unknown as they wrestle with the big and small questions of their lives and God's part in them. Although what they know may be incomplete, it is not insignificant.

If we desire to assist older children in their quest for God, we will do well to follow Coles's lead. Get to know the children with whom you live and work, let them become comfortable with you as a friend, and then listen to discover where they see God at work, what they understand, and the questions they are asking about God. We can help children get better acquainted with biblical characters and encourage their interest in and their relationship with Jesus. We can also bless children by taking seriously what God is saying to them and believing that God is at work in their lives.

Seven

GROWING IN FAITH

hree-year-old Junior scurried up the steps, ran to the edge of the deck, and shouted, "Daddy, Daddy." As Daddy turned in his direction, Junior ordered, "Catch me." The little body went tense; he prepared for the big risk; he jumped; and he landed safely in his daddy's arms. His face lit up with a big smile, and giggling with glee, he squirmed to get down and do it again. You have probably watched similar scenes many times. This fun, the excitement of the risk, is possible because Junior has complete faith in his father.

FAITH DEFINED

Faith—what is it? We use the word freely, referring to the faith we have in a person, a company, an institution, or an elevator. The word *faith* shows up frequently when we talk about religion or the spiritual life. But what meanings does the word carry? Often for common words we have a general understanding of their meaning, picked up somewhere in our past but never examined. Before looking specifically at the faith of children, it will be helpful to explore the biblical meaning of faith.

The apostle Paul in his preaching and writing often spoke of faith in God or faith in Christ Jesus.[1] Hebrews 11:1 defines faith as "the assurance of things hoped for, the conviction of things not seen." Biblical faith is not some feeling that stands alone; rather, it is the deeply felt and held assurance of God's faithfulness and power. It is confidence in the willingness and the ability of Jesus to bring us into a relationship with God and to empower us to live the Christian life. One's faith must be in a faithful object,[2] or faith is nothing but wishful thinking. Faith is also the response of human beings to God's promises and love; however, we do not initiate our response. Paul stated that our faith response to grace, which results in salvation, is a gift from God (Eph. 2:8). As we will see, many factors influence our faith, but Christian faith always has in it the gift of God at work initiating faith and making it possible.

Quoting the Old Testament prophet Habakkuk, Paul declared, "The one who is righteous will live by faith" (Rom. 1:17; Gal. 3:11). Our trust in God is to order our lives and influence every part of who we are and what we do. Christians are to live and grow by faith. A common faith unifies people, bonds them together, and gives them a shared mission on which to work. Paul begged the Ephesians to live in unity and indicated this was possible because they had one Lord, one faith, and one baptism. Paul was confident that as the Christians were equipped to do God's work and as they began to build one another up, they would come to unity of faith (Eph. 4:1–6, 12–13). There is also the inference here that faith changes as persons learn and grow in the faith community.

Contemporary Christian educators and scholars have taken a deep interest in how people come to faith and then understand and live their faith. James W. Fowler is one who has made the study of faith the focus of his life's work. He examined the process of having faith and identified characteristics of the process that are used by persons of different religions—Christianity, Judaism, Islam, or secular humanism for example. Fowler examined the faith of children, youth, and adults and identified specific changes in faith as it developed.

Fowler offers a three-part definition of faith. In his definition we see some parallels to the biblical faith discussed briefly above. Fowler sees faith as:

1. A dynamic pattern of personal trust in and loyalty to a center or centers of value.
2. Trust in and loyalty to images and realities of power.
3. Trust in and loyalty to a shared master story or core story.[3]

Trust and loyalty are the foundation of faith or the threads woven through all dimensions of faith.

A *center of value* is a power that is much bigger than we are, someone or something beyond us, the transcendent one. We are devoted to and love whatever becomes our center of value and find meaning as we live our lives focused on and guided by that central value. In the Christian faith, the ultimate center of value is to be the Creator, the redeemer God. If we truly live the Christian faith, God will be the focus of our trust, loyalty, and love. We will understand the meaning of our lives in terms of God's activity on our behalf and of our involvement in God's plans. Our center of value is the object of our faith.

When you picture the ultimate power on which you depend, what do you see? The psalmist David said, "The LORD is my shepherd, I shall not want" (Ps. 23:1). David's *image of power* or picture of the one he trusted and to whom he gave his loyalty was the Lord of the universe gently and wisely shepherding sheep. That image provided him with a deep sense of security. David knew what a good shepherd did, and he was convinced he could count on God to be his Good Shepherd and to supply all his needs. Psalm twenty-three paints the detailed picture of David's faith, his assurance of what he hoped for, his conviction of what was yet unseen.

> The LORD is my shepherd, I shall not want.
> He makes me lie down in green pastures;
> he leads me beside still waters;
> he restores my soul.
> He leads me in right paths
> for his name's sake.
> Even though I walk through the darkest valley,
> I fear no evil;
> for you are with me;
> your rod and your staff—
> they comfort me.

You prepare a table before me
    in the presence of my enemies;
you anoint my head with oil;
    my cup overflows.
Surely goodness and mercy shall follow me
    all the days of my life,
and I shall dwell in the house of the LORD
    my whole life long.

Psalm 23:1–6

Other images of God also nourished David's faith. In Psalm 131:2 we read:

But I have calmed and quieted my soul,
    like a weaned child with its mother;
    my soul is like the weaned child that is with me.

David saw himself in the arms of his mother, not hungrily seeking for food, but simply enjoying the presence and love of his mother.[4] His image of the Lord was that of a loving, enfolding mother. He also pictured God as a compassionate father: "As a father has compassion for his children, so the LORD has compassion for those who fear him" (Ps. 103:13). Another time the Lord was David's ideal parent who would be there if his inadequate, fallible human parents let him down: "If my father and mother forsake me, the LORD will take me up" (Ps. 27:10). In Psalm 96:10–13, David proclaimed the Lord as king and judge.

Say among the nations, "The LORD is king!
    The world is firmly established; it shall never be moved.
    He will judge the peoples with equity."
Let the heavens be glad, and let the earth rejoice;
    let the sea roar, and all that fills it;
    let the field exult, and everything in it.
Then shall all the trees of the forest sing for joy
    before the LORD; for he is coming,
    for he is coming to judge the earth.
He will judge the world with righteousness, and the peoples with his
    truth.

The coming of this king would cause great joy for he would bring order and stability, equity and righteous judgments. David, the poet, seems to have thought in images and filled his writing with these and many other pictures of God. They let us see the kind of God in whom David placed his faith.

Our images of God color our faith with bright splashes of joy and love, subtle hues of confidence, comfort, and peace, or dark shades of distrust, fear, and aloneness. With David we may picture God as the Good Shepherd, a loving parent, and a wise, faithful king and judge. Or we may see God as a stern and distant father, an undependable mother, or an unpleaseable judge. How can one trust in or be loyal to those latter images? Is it any wonder that many persons find it very difficult to have faith? Our image of God is a crucial part of our faith, and the images of God our children are forming will greatly influence their faith.

Faith includes not only a center of value and an image of power but, thirdly, trust in and loyalty to a story that helps us make sense out of our world and experiences. This is what Fowler calls the *shared master story*. A master story—called a worldview by some—gives answers to the most basic questions humans seek to answer: Who am I? Where am I? What is wrong? What is the solution?

For Christians the master story is the story of the Bible. Through our master story we come to know God and continue to form our images of God.[5] We discover God's purpose for creating us, how God wants us to live, and what it means to be good. Stories within the master story often stimulate a desire to be like the characters in the story and often give the courage to follow their examples.[6] The master story we trust in and are loyal to is the lens through which we see everything and through which persons and events are given their meaning.[7]

Fowler's three elements of faith—a center of value, image of power, and master story—are interrelated. Earlier we discussed the impact of our image of God on our ability to trust in God as our center of value. Our image of God also predisposes us to see certain things as we read the Bible—the master story. If our God is an all-powerful king, doing what he pleases and not having to answer to anyone else for his actions, biblical events demonstrating the power of God will impress us. We may skip over evidence of God's gentleness and love without noticing it. Among Christians who turn to the Bible as the source of our master story, we find varying understandings of God and how God works in the lives of people and in the world. Our image of God influences the story we discover. On the other hand, as we hear the biblical story told by persons with a somewhat different image of God, or if we explore the Scripture more thoroughly or with the capacities and needs of a new level of development, the story can correct, expand, and refine our image of God, deepening our trust in God.

Note that Fowler speaks of a *shared* master story. Persons do not have faith in isolation. Faith is experienced in a community that shares a trust in and loyalty to the same master story. Fowler believes that faith is a three-way covenantal relationship, which involves a trusting commitment between God, the self, and others. When we have a shared faith in God and in the master story of God's working in the world, our commitment to one another becomes deeper. As we learn and explore the stories of our faith together, our trust in God grows stronger.[8]

STAGES OF FAITH

Informed by developmental understandings from Erikson, Piaget, and Kohlberg, James Fowler began his research of faith development. He found that as individuals coped constructively with the challenges and crises of life described by Erikson, the needed faith formed to allow for constructive coping. The functioning of an appropriate form of faith is necessary for ordering and finding meaning in each period of life. Since the challenges change and become more complex throughout life, faith must change also if it is to be sufficient. With each new level of development, persons have new capacities for relating to and trusting one another along with new potentials for a relationship with God. God created human beings with the capacity and the deep need to have faith.[9] Without faith, life is a lonely, meaningless existence.

As with other developmental potentials, faith does not automatically unfold, but God intended for trust and loyalty to develop in relationships with others. Children are born with readiness for faith but need an environment of mutual love, care, and interaction for the faith potential to become a reality. Fowler believes that when an environment of warm responsiveness surrounds infants they "show a strong predisposition to grow toward healthy relationships and toward construction of a coherent and life sustaining sense of faith and meaning."[10] From his research, Fowler described the path persons follow as this life-sustaining faith develops. He identified one prestage and six qualitatively different stages or ways of having faith. In this chapter we will examine the sections of the faith journey where we are most likely to find children.

Primal Faith

Fowler's understanding of primal faith grows out of Erikson's description of the first life crisis—trust versus mistrust. *Primal faith* is a basic disposition to trust. In relationships with their parents, siblings, and other caregiving adults, babies form trust and loyalties or they come to mistrust their world and withdraw. We have already seen how the responsive care and the faithful return of parents and other caregivers help babies develop trust. They first trust their mother and the nurturing environment she creates. When they feel loved and enjoyed, they come to trust themselves as worthy of being loved. This basic trust is the embryo of faith, which can come to maturity in a relationship with God.[11]

Fowler believes primal faith most likely has its beginning even before birth. As parents anticipate with joy the arrival of their little one, the sense of being wanted and cherished quite possibly can be communicated to the unborn child. Being cherished sets the stage for trust, and it is in the family that trust grows. When the faith of family members is real, it permeates who they are; they surround the baby with faith as they love, care for, and play with the infant. Babies begin to hear parents and older siblings pray, sing, or talk about God before they have any awareness of what the words mean. As soon as they sit in their high chair and join the family at meals, many children are taught to fold their hands and bow their heads as the family thanks God for the food. Often this becomes a fun game that brings praise when the baby learns the ritual. In all these events the child is being introduced to God and begins to build into his or her memory the feelings, sights, and sounds experienced when God is mentioned.[12]

According to Fowler, this memory-building activity is the beginning of imagination. When babies are capable of taking the feelings, sights, sounds, and smells experienced as they interact with other people or things and construct them into a memory or image of the event, they are using their imagination. As little ones begin to form their image of God, imagination is the tool they use.[13]

Rituals aid in the process of forming the memories that bring comfort and pleasure. As parents care for their baby, that care often falls into a pattern—a ritual—that seems to be the best way of doing things. Babies remember the repeated pattern and find comfort in knowing what to expect.

Rituals also show up in the games we play with infants. We soon discover that babies love to do things again and again and again. Through these rituals they learn how to participate in interactions with others.[14] We throw the blanket over the baby's head and ask, "Where's Tiffany?" Quickly lifting the blanket we exclaim, "Oh, there she is," and then begin again. Each time, a smiling Tiffany appears from under the blanket to greet our surprised smile. She will remember the fun and in the future will respond joyously to the prospect of this simple ritual. Soon she will initiate the game herself, covering her own head and waiting to hear, "Where's Tiffany?" This comfort and joy in ritual prepares the way for later satisfying experiences with God through meaningful rituals of the faith.

Primal faith forms before children have language to describe it and before they are actually conscious of the worth and trust they feel. However, the influence of this first basic faith is critical, even though we have no memory of its forming. Fowler states, "although it does not determine the course of our later faith, it lays the foundation on which later faith will build or that will have to be rebuilt in later faith."[15] Basic trust is the essential foundation for faith in God. If that basic trust does not form in infancy or is destroyed later in life, trust must be built or rebuilt before a person can come to a life-sustaining faith in God.

Intuitive-Projective Faith

Around the age of two, as children begin using language to represent their experiences and to communicate, they begin to develop what Fowler calls *intuitive-projective faith*. This faith stage usually continues until the age of six or seven and is a time when children form their faith intuitively rather than with formal logic.[16] Because of the egocentric nature of their thinking, young children tend to project their own meanings into events without questioning whether they have it right. As we have already said, the first conscious images of God form during these early childhood years. Stories, gestures of a pastor or other significant adult conducting a religious ritual, and symbols such as lighted candles or a picture seen at church stimulate the imagination of children. They picture the event or the story as they imaginatively perceive it and combine with that picture the strong feelings stimulated by the story or the event to form an image that has a long-lasting influence on their faith.[17]

Characteristics of Intuitive-Projective Faith

During early childhood, children learn they can do things for themselves, take the initiative, decide what they want to do, and do it. Children who are affirmed by loving adults when they express autonomy and initiative, rather than being shamed or made to feel guilty, develop a healthy sense of their worth and abilities. They incorporate into their image of God this affirming love of parents and their sense of being lovable. The result is a faith characterized by a "robust sense of being held in the care and love of God."[18] That strong sense of God's loving care is the faith young children need.

When preschool children think about God and how God works, they think in concrete pictures and from their perspective. Matthew lived in the same town as his grandma and grandpa Long and was with them often. A few months before he was born, Matthew's maternal grandfather, Grandpa Riffle, died. One day when he was about two years old, after being with Grandma Riffle, he asked, "Where is Grandma Riffle's daddy?" His mother answered, "Grandpa Riffle is in heaven with Jesus." Brightly, Matthew responded, "I'm going to heaven someday. Yep, I'm going to play with Jesus. I'm going to play with Jesus' toys." Matthew, at a very early age, had a positive image of being with Jesus—an image that was concrete and constructed out of the stuff of childhood.

Young children are also great imitators. They watch parents, older siblings, and other significant adults and mimic what they do. As they seek to be like these important people, children are "powerfully and permanently influenced" by how these significant others live their lives and their faith, by their moods, and by the stories they tell of their faith.[19]

My friend Mary once told me, "Little Jim and Little Mary stories were favorites for our children." As we tell our children stories from our lives, do we include faith stories? Do we share memories of early experiences of God or of pleasant events in the faith community? Children will also profit from hearing how God responds to our prayers and how God meets our needs in the present. It is natural for them to follow our lead, to do what they see us doing in life and in the stories we tell.

The Role of Imagination in Intuitive-Projective Faith

Several factors contribute to faith development during early childhood. Imagination is at work in the forming of intuitive-projective faith. As children stretch to understand God's involvement in their experiences and in their world, they call on their imagination to provide explanations or answers for questions they had never thought about before. Often their explanations are magical.[20]

One morning at the breakfast table four-year-old Laura announced, "Jesus isn't in my heart anymore." "Oh?" her mother responded. "Yesterday after I hurt my foot, I asked Jesus to make it better," Laura explained. "So he walked down my leg and into my foot to make it better. So he's not in my heart anymore." Using imagination, Laura created what was for her a totally satisfactory explanation of how Jesus functions.

The root meaning of *imagination* is the "power" of "forming."[21] Imagination is the power to form in our minds the images of reality. Fowler sees imagination as a powerful force in all learning not just in faith development. When young children use imagination to form their image of God, they are using a natural tool for learning. Not only is imagination—imaging—important to children, it is also important to adults. We, too, need concrete symbols—images—to remind us of our faith. I am not speaking here of idols to be worshiped but of symbols that draw us into an experience with God. Such symbols are present in most if not all branches of Christianity.[22] At the Last Supper, Jesus gave us such symbols:

Then he took a loaf of bread, and when he had given thanks, he broke it and gave it to them, saying, "This is my body, which is given for you. Do this in remembrance of me." And he did the same with the cup after supper, saying, "This cup that is poured out for you is the new covenant in my blood."

Luke 22:19–20

Each time we come to the Lord's Table, as we take the concrete symbols of bread and wine, we reenact the Last Supper and remember that Christ died for us. Through this symbolic act we meet and remember Christ anew.

The Salvation Army is one denomination that does not use the concrete symbols of bread and wine for observing the sacrament of communion, but their expression of faith is not without symbols. Salvation Army Christians are called soldiers, and all members wear uniforms symbolizing that they are members of God's army, seeking to bring God's kingdom on earth.

Quakers believe that the concrete symbols of bread and wine are not needed for communion with Christ, therefore, they also do not observe the sacrament of communion. Most Quaker congregations, however, have a quiet time of communion each Sunday morning—a period of silence for each person to commune with God and to share a message of encouragement or challenge with the congregation if the Spirit moves them to do so. This, too, is a symbol. Our church buildings are also symbols of our faith, whether in their simplicity or in their display of faith symbols.

As children construct their understandings of God and religion, they are surrounded by symbols for their imaginations to take hold of and to build into their faith images. When children begin to ask questions about the rituals and symbols of the faith, we know their imaginations are grasped by the symbol and that they are working to create a meaning for it. This is the time to tell the child the story of the ritual's meaning and to tell the story of how you met God in the ritual or of times when a symbol reminded you of God. The imaginations of children, we must remember, are not working just when they ask questions. Images begin to form out of vague feelings and inner responses that are below the level of consciousness. By the time children ask their questions, some elements of their image are already in place, and the imagination blends together the new information given with the deep feelings and the previous perceptions of the child.[23]

For symbols of the faith to contribute to the child's inner images and for adults to be able to share the meanings of the symbols, young children and adults must regularly be together in the presence of those symbols, participating in the rituals. No matter what we say to them, however, we do not give children our understanding of the symbols. They construct their own images, which are a combination of deep feelings, quite accurate pictures, fanciful but harmless perceptions, and possibly some destructive assumptions. Adults of faith who are in a relationship with children and are listening to them will discover some of the distortions and will be able to help the children make corrections in the image. As children develop, they will need to continue reflecting on their faith images.[24]

Young children are dramatic and playful. They spend hours acting out the flow of events their imaginations create. Much of this dramatic play is their experimentation with the world they observe and with the roles of the people in it. When children have seen only a small piece of life, yet know there is more, a sense of mystery draws them to that segment of life. For example, children see parents leave the house each weekday with an attaché case, a tool chest, or in a uniform. What happens next is a mystery to children, and they explore the edges of that mystery by playing "going to work."

This love of the dramatic, the fascination with mystery, and the desire to explore it prepare children to participate in the rituals of the faith.[25] The Old Testament Jewish tradition was rich with both family and faith community rituals in which children participated. Children in Christian families today can be assisted in their faith development as they, too, participate with adults in rituals that capture their faith story. Young children will not be able to explain the meaning of the ritual, but experiencing it may provide important pieces to be incorporated into their images of God and faith.

Stories in Intuitive-Projective Faith

Anyone who associates with young children knows they love stories. Preschoolers can be captivated by short stories, and four- to six-year-old children can enjoy listening to quite lengthy ones. They seldom do well, though, at retelling stories in detail and in sequence.[26]

They know when we change or skip a line in their favorite books, but their minds are not yet able to reconstruct all the pieces of the story in order. Through imagination, children enter stories and live them; they are entertained by the story and as they live the stories, they learn about life and possibly goodness and God. Faith stories that capture the imagination of a child can awaken and shape beliefs, values, and loyalties that take deep root in the child's heart.

In *Stages of Faith*, Fowler tells of a four-year-old child whose mother read a Bible story to him every afternoon before his nap. One of his favorite stories was Daniel in the lions' den. When the story ended and his mother had left the room, he often relived that dramatic situation. He remembers that on at least one occasion he thought to himself, as though saying it out loud, "God, I'm brave like Daniel. Put some lions here in this room, and I will show you that I am not afraid." Then, he said, he began to feel real fright at the possibility that God might really do what he asked.[27] The imagination of this four-year-old discovered bravery as a great value. He wanted to be brave and to prove that he could be bravely loyal to God by facing great danger, just like Daniel.

Fowler believes that young children find comfort in stories where good prevails and, in the end, evil people must pay for their sins. Stories can articulate the inner fears of children and can show them how to deal with those fears and the strong impulses they feel to do what they believe is wrong. When in the story those who stand for good win, children are assured that they, too, will have the strength to win over danger and evil.[28] Many Bible stories give children the opportunity to see God as the one who helps people gain such victories.

Some child psychologists and educators have proposed rewriting fairy tales to take out the violence and would also want to protect young children from many biblical dramas. They believe children's stories should carry only messages of sweetness, harmony, and love. But others believe children need stories that bring out into the open the often unspeakable fears that haunt children and picture the conquering of those fears. This does not mean that hours spent alone or with other children in front of the television watching violence equips a child to deal with the dark side of life. The exposure of children "to death, poverty, treachery and maliciousness in the context of fairy tales and Bible stories" will be constructive only "when told to them by trusted adults with whom their feelings can be tested and shared."[29]

Fears and Intuitive-Projective Faith

Around the age of three or four many children develop a fear of death—especially the death of their parents.[30] When I was a preschooler, one day my father was joking around and took a handful of flour and turned his black hair gray. I burst into tears; he had touched my deep fear that he would grow old and die. As children struggle with this fear, they need adults who will listen to their questions, provide honest answers, and assure them of God's love in every situation. Through the search for honest, assuring answers, simple enough to give comfort to a child, we will grow in faith.

As toddlers begin to express their autonomy, they discover that certain activities are forbidden. Parents can set boundaries for what is and is not allowed and can administer negative consequences when children get out of bounds and do the forbidden. Children are soon aware when they have done what they have been told not to do and can feel shame for "being the rebellious one . . . lured into" the prohibited.[31] In this awareness of the forbidden and in the experience of shame, a sense of sin begins to form. Young children need adults to lovingly set boundaries for their protection and to provide judgment and consequences that keep them within those protective boundaries. In this structure, children find security. When children experience shame for what they have done, they need release. Release comes when they take the established consequences—time out on a chair or being deprived of a privilege—and then receive assurance of the parent's love and forgiveness. Since young children see God as the ultimate parent, they expect God to set limits and to punish those who violate those limits. It is important for them to know that God also forgives.

The child's active imagination is the great strength at work in intuitive-projective faith. With imagination children can construct powerful, sustaining images of God. But imagination is also a danger since children are capable of creating powerful, terrorizing images of God. Adults sometimes exploit children, feeding their imagination with fear-inducing images to keep their behavior in line; some even threaten children with God's wrath if they misbehave. Such actions do great harm to children and their faith. Preschoolers need the security of faith in a loving, faithful God who holds them. A God who sets limits, yes, but only out of love and for their protection.

Parents and teachers have the responsibility and the privilege of giving children stories rich in positive images of God, goodness, and courage and of introducing them to symbols and rituals that point to God's faithfulness, love, and protection. We can also give the gift of creating an environment in which children have the opportunity to express their fears and questions and to talk about the images of God they are forming.[32]

Mythic-Literal Faith

Around the age of six or seven, children begin to develop a *mythic-literal faith*, which continues to form during the elementary and into the middle school years. Fowler in his research also found some adolescents and adults using mythic-literal faith.[33] A myth is a traditional story that explains origins, customs, religious practices, and the activities of the gods. In naming mythic-literal faith, Fowler highlighted the important role of story—myth—and the literal character of the thinking in this faith stage.

Characteristics of Mythic-Literal Faith

The development of the capacity for concrete logical thought makes possible this new stage or form of faith.[34] Most school-age children understand the working of cause and effect and the ordering of events in sequence. What they know is no longer just a collection of perceptions; they begin to see relationships and to logically link their pieces of knowledge. Elementary children have a desire to figure out how things work and to know what is really true. This leads them to sort out the imaginary from the real—to check perceptions and to see whether things are as they seem to be. As they become interested in what is real, children still enjoy using their imaginations, but imagination is usually confined to play, and the children do not confuse make-believe with reality.[35]

For children in the mythic-literal faith stage, their image of God is in transition. When Fowler asked Millie what God looked like, she answered, "Well, I don't know. But do you want me to tell you what I imagine he looks like?" She then proceeded to describe an anthropo-morphic picture of God. Millie questioned the accuracy of her image of God, realizing that he may not be a person with a concrete body, but she still pictured God that way and her imagination continued to serve her as she thought about God.[36]

Mythic-literal faith requires that children be able to see things from another person's point of view. They can choose to look at a situation from another person's perspective and see how the perspective is sim-ilar to or different from their own.[37] Children are limited in the range of perspectives that they can comprehend. They most easily under-stand the viewpoint of people like themselves—their family, friends, and those whose experiences are similar to theirs. Even as children try to see the world as others see it, their perspective is colored by their own needs, interests, and wishes. Children are not yet able to reflect on the inner working of their thoughts and desires and are therefore unaware of how their needs, interests, and wishes control them. They are also unable to think about the inner life of others. They cannot consciously set aside their inner motives and consider the other's needs or wishes without being influenced by their own.[38]

A mythic-literal faith understands justice in terms of reciprocity—an equal exchange. Children are very concerned about what is fair, and by that they mean equal treatment. Reciprocity may involve an exchange of favors, appropriate rewards for good behavior, or appro-priate punishment for bad behavior. They believe this reciprocal exchange is built into the very nature of things. Put another way, they believe in imminent justice; God who is the creator of the nature of things will certainly act justly, with reciprocity.

Out of this strong belief in reciprocity and the concrete literalism of the child's thinking comes the view of God as a powerful parent or ruler who is stern but fair. God can be counted on both to reward good behavior and to punish those who are bad. Even a forgiving God, they believe, must preserve fairness by punishing those who do wrong, even when their intentions were good. From such a view of God, some children become perfectionists, working very hard to be good; they understand righteousness as doing the right things. Those who fail in their effort to be good may develop a deep sense of being bad and conclude that they are incapable of being good.

Children may also fear that God will leave them if they do not keep up their end of the bargain. Such a fear may haunt the child who begins to question past beliefs and finds them inadequate but has yet to discover new ways of believing in God. As children develop the ability to take the perspective of others, they are able to see God as one who can and does take their perspective. A God who sees things from their point of view can be compassionate. This compassion, however, is combined with the image of the wise, firm parent who in fairness must reward and punish.[39]

The Role of Story in Mythic-Literal Faith

School-age children become storytellers. Not only do they enjoy hearing stories, they can look back over the events of their lives and weave those events together into a story or narrative and, in the process, discover meaning in those concrete experiences. With the ability to create their stories, children can communicate to others their experiences and the meaning they see in them.[40] As they tell their stories and listen to the stories of others, they can make comparisons and learn more about life. Elementary children also do well at retelling stories they have heard.

Stories are at the heart of faith development for children; stories capture and communicate theology for them. When adults try to explain God to children in abstract characteristics, even using simple, everyday language, the teaching does not carry meaning for them. But children can know God from stories and can experience God in stories.[41]

One day nine-year-old John and I sat enjoying pizza when I asked, "John, what have you learned about God that you think other children should know?" He answered, "Oh, I haven't learned hardly anything about God." John's parents are strong Christians, deeply committed to their children, and John regularly participated in all the church ministries with children. Had both home and church failed miserably in teaching him about God?

Later in our conversation I asked, "John, have you ever felt God near?" Without a moment of hesitation and with excitement in his voice he responded, "Yes. Like, when I was thinking about Adam and Eve in the garden and how they sinned and God gave them a second chance. Oh, I know they paid for their sins and all, but God gave them a second chance. And Noah [he meant Jonah] when he ran away. God gave him a second chance."

In these Old Testament stories John discovered the God of second chances. That knowledge of God was so meaningful that he felt God close to him when he thought of those stories. When I asked the abstract question about God, John had nothing to tell me. But when I asked about his experience of God, he could tell me the stories that captured one of the most significant things he knew about God.

John demonstrates that children not only remember the facts and sequence of the events in stories but are also able to discover meaning in them. The meanings children see are concrete, literal, and usually connected with only one level of the story's possible meaning.[42] Even though, from an adult perspective, their concrete, one-dimensional meanings are limited, they may be profoundly significant for the child. John is a bright, active, sociable child who believes that people are for enjoying. When others are around, he goes into an "enjoy people mode" whether in a class session or at a party. It is almost impossible for him to keep his body still, even when he is listening intently. Children like John are often in trouble at school, church, and home for not fitting into the expectations of the setting. John needed to know a God of second chances, and he met that God in the stories of Scripture. The meaning he saw in the biblical narratives connected with the concrete reality of his life and drew him to God. Stories, drama, and other symbols powerfully influence children.

In the elementary school years, children begin to take ownership of the stories, beliefs, and religious rituals valued by those who belong to their faith communities.[43] Their identity in the community grows as they learn the stories, recite some of the beliefs, and participate in the rituals—when they can say, "This is what *we* believe, what *we* do. This is *our* story."

Jewish children are more likely than Protestant children to have this sense of identity. Grace remembers learning this many years ago. As a five-year-old she invited a little Jewish girlfriend home to dinner. When Grace's mother brought the apple pie to the table, the young visitor asked, "Is the pie made with lard?" When told it was, she responded, "Thank you, but I won't have any then." The little girl was content to let the family eat their pie while she had none because she knew that they were different from her. They were Christians, she was a Jew, and dietary observances set Jews apart from Christians. At five years of age she owned the rituals that symbolized her faith community and had the strength to observe them even when it meant being different.

As noted earlier, the Old Testament instructed Jewish parents to place religious symbols on the door frames of the house and through weekly and annual rituals to tell the stories of how God brought the people of Israel into existence. These symbols, rituals, and stories helped to form the identity of the children.

Our children need the stories that capture and communicate to them the distinctiveness of our faith community. They need to hear stories that carry the core beliefs of the community. Biblical narratives provide the basic set of stories containing the important Christian beliefs, and children receive a great gift when we tell them Bible stories with clarity and drama. They also need to hear the stories of their particular faith tradition. For example, John Wesley, father of Methodism, nearly died at the age of six. Just seconds before the flaming thatched roof of his home fell in on his bedroom, the men of the community made a human ladder so that one of them could reach young John and lift him from the window ledge. John Wesley always believed he was a "brand plucked from the burning" to do some special work for God. Through Wesley's story, children today can begin to believe that God still has work for them to do.

In 1860 when a group of reformers, recently excommunicated from the Methodist Church, met to form a new denomination, they chose a name that captured their basic commitments. They were Methodists who believed in certain freedoms, therefore they called themselves Free Methodists. Freedom for slaves was very important to them. Do Free Methodist children today know the stories of Free Methodists who worked with the underground railroad assisting slaves in their escape to Canada and freedom? Have they heard how the first bishop of the church sent everyone home from camp meeting early so that they could cast their vote against legalizing slavery in Illinois?

As children hear and own such stories, they can begin to develop an identity as one who stands against prejudice and anything that oppresses others. Denominations, local churches, and families need to keep alive the stories that communicate who they are and what they believe. Those stories give our children basic beliefs that they will want to own and help them develop a faith identity, which gives them a sense of belonging.

Synthetic-Conventional Faith

Between the ages of eleven and fifteen, older children or early adolescents begin to develop what Fowler calls *synthetic-conventional faith.* Although for most it is the faith stage of adolescence, the transition into this new stage begins for some children during the middle school years. By the onset of puberty the brain has developed to the point where formal abstract thought and deeper reflection are possible. An expanding sphere of social relationships brings children into contact with persons whose master stories or basic beliefs conflict with theirs. In the face of these conflicting perspectives, children use their developing thought processes to reflect more deeply on the meaning of their master stories and their faith. This reflection leads to the beginning of synthetic-conventional faith[44]—a faith constructed by synthesizing meanings, beliefs, and values received from various sectors of their world. The conventions or accepted standards of their peer group, society, church, and family are the givens with which older children and adolescents work as they form their faith.

Characteristics of Synthetic-Conventional Faith

As children move toward adolescence, interpersonal relationships become increasingly important to them. They want to invest more time with friends and less with family. Many young teens have a special chum with whom they spend immense amounts of time just being together and talking. Through these seemingly endless conversations in which they share their inner thoughts and feelings, friends gain their first conscious experiences of being known, understood, and accepted, which brings great satisfaction. On the other hand, these same teens suffer deep pain when they are misunderstood and rejected.[45]

The ability to use abstract thought makes it possible for young people to think about others thinking about them. As they use this new ability, they become acutely aware of what friends, parents, teachers, and others who are significant expect of them. Meeting those expectations so that one continues to be accepted becomes a driving force and leads the adolescent to be a conformist. As they conform, they build into their faith structure the conventional values and beliefs of those most significant to them.[46]

Since interpersonal relationships are a central value for early adolescents, it is no surprise that God is understood in terms of an extension of human relationships. As synthetic-conventional faith forms, many young people experience a deep hunger for a personal relationship with God. They want to be known and accepted by the one who can know them more fully than anyone else. And they long for acceptance from God that affirms the worth of their personhood. When we present God as one who offers companionship, guidance, and love, early adolescents desire to know and be known by that God.[47] For young people who enter into a personal relationship with God, God becomes a significant other—possibly the most significant other—whom they desire to please. Their lives are powerfully influenced by what they understand as God's expectations—the values, beliefs, and commitments to which God calls them.

Community and Synthetic-Conventional Faith

North Americans glorify individualism and self-chosen beliefs. Many voices call for a value-free environment in which children and youth learn and make their own choices without external influence. Many others believe such an environment is impossible. If a value-free environment could be created, it would not be a setting in which the forming of the faith of children and adolescents would be enhanced. Fowler found that young people construct their first articulate, self-defining belief system through conforming to the values and standards of others rather than by independently forming their own system.[48] Older children need a community of peers and adults with whom to begin forming a synthetic-conventional faith and to begin establishing for themselves a set of values, beliefs, and commitments that will guide their decision making and energize their wills to live out those commitments—a community that knows and lives its faith.

Drawing older children into such a community and helping them develop a sense of belonging and ownership in it is crucial to continued faith development throughout adolescence. Sometimes children who participated fully in the life of the church during the elementary years fail to make the transition into the youth group and drift away from the faith community. This often happens with children who do not establish close friendships with peers in the church. When working with children in the church, watch for the socially isolated children and seek to help them build bonds of friendship within the faith community. Those involved with children's ministries and youth ministries should plan together for the transition into youth group so that the young newcomers are welcomed and all are assisted in developing a sense of belonging.

As children move into adolescence, they need a community that provides "stories, ideas, belief systems, rituals, disciplines, and role models that can capture and fund their imaginations and hunger for adult truth."[49] In addition to peer friendships, older children and adolescents need friendships with adults in the faith community. The potential for faith development is enhanced when young people spend time with adults who themselves are maturing in faith. Youth discover the values and beliefs of adults who invest time and energy in them over several months or years. They want to be like these significant adults and will conform to many of their beliefs and values. It is important that these adults are persons of integrity, living what they teach and growing in their understanding of God and in their grasp of the master story of their faith.

PROCESS AND CRISIS IN FAITH

We see continuity in what is needed to facilitate the forming of faith from stage to stage. Stories, rituals, discipline, and interaction with adults who are caring, growing persons of faith continue to be essential for faith development. Methods used by older children to dig into biblical stories may change. They are ready to explore more seriously the meanings of rituals and to participate in special rituals appropriate for their place on the journey of life. Their friendships with adults take on new dimensions as the young people become more responsible, work on projects with adults, and share in discussing thoughts and feelings. Methods and dynamics change, but story, ritual, relationships, and the energizing of the imagination—the image of what can be—remain the basics for the forming and transforming of faith.

To this point our discussion has focused on the gradual process of faith development, which is not the whole picture. Fowler refers to faith development as a dance that has "twin movements of maturation and development on one hand, and of recentering and transformation in Christ, on the other."[50] Faith involves development and conversion—both are essential. Development prepares the way for conversion as the image of God forms and children learn the stories that make God known. But the time must come when persons choose God as the center of their life, when they trust Christ to transform them and make it possible for them to live the Christian life. For some, conversion is a dramatic transforming experience after a period of having ignored God and having put their trust in themselves and in false hopes. For others, particularly sensitive children who began responding to God at an early age, conversion involves times of deepening commitment as they come to better know God and themselves.

When accompanying children on the faith journey, adults must be sensitive to their readiness for response and must never try to force children into an early conversion experience. Some adults emphasize the child's sinfulness and fear of hell in an attempt to bring children to conversion. Responding out of fear before they have the inner desire for a deeper commitment to God often results in a rigid faith of external authority rather than in a trusting relationship with God in which the person experiences ongoing transformation and maturing.[51]

On the other hand, children do develop a sense of sinfulness and need to know that they can be forgiven. In settings where adults are invited to respond to God, some children will also want to respond. When children are told that Jesus wants to be their special friend and Savior, some will be ready to enter that relationship. Adults must never discourage a child who desires to respond to God. When children know that God invites them to come and they are ready for a response, they do not need severe external pressure. They simply need a setting for response and possibly an adult to guide them, pray with them, and affirm their encounter with God.

Conversion is not the end of the faith journey. Faith development and refining must continue through the changes of life so that faith is not out of step with development in other areas. Children are created with the potential for faith development, and we have the privilege of helping to release that potential. Each faith stage is to be valued and experienced fully as a necessary part of the faith forming process. When faith keeps step with other aspects of human development, faith will be adequate for each period of life and will be transformed to meet the needs of the next developmental phase.[52]

Eight

SETTING THE STAGE FOR KNOWING GOD

On a Sunday morning in July the pastor announced, "We still have staffing needs for this fall in our children's ministries. We need a director for the midweek Club House program, teachers for first- and fifth-grade Sunday school classes, and several nursery workers. Join me in praying that God will provide a full team to minister with our children. And if you sense God calling you to serve in any of these areas, contact me or Grace Abbott, our director of Christian education."

Similar announcements may have been made in hundreds of churches on that same Sunday. Recruiting people to work with children seems to be a never-ending task for Christian education leaders. Millions of volunteers minister every week with children in local churches around the world. How valuable are these structured times of religious instruction? Are the time and energy of the volunteers wisely invested, or should a few persons instruct young adults in Christian parenting and let the parents of the children nurture their faith informally in the home? The nurture provided by parents is of primary importance, but I believe structured ministries with children in the church also have a significant role to play.

"All children," says Walter Wangerin Jr., "experience the Dear Almighty. All people begin, at least, to dance with Deity. And yet so few continue in the dance. . . . And why? Because, when they needed language to name and to save the experience, it was not given unto them. . . . No system came to cradle the truth of their experience. Therefore, the experience fell into discredit, together with their lisps."[1]

To live and grow, faith needs religion. Children—and adolescents or adults with a newborn faith—must learn God's name and the stories of God's people. They must join with others in rituals that express and affirm their faith. Through planned Christian education ministries, communities of faith can help children discover the language to name their experiences with God and a religious system or tradition to cradle the truth of those experiences. This chapter will examine the functioning of religious language and give one example of how the stage may be set for children to meet God and to have their faith cradled.

RELIGIOUS LANGUAGE

Religious language gives us words, narratives, and parables that help us to make sense of our experiences with God, to come to know God better, and to make meaning of what we experience and learn in all of life. Through religious language we may draw near to God and experience God's presence. Religious language takes various forms, which Jerome Berryman refers to as different layers of language.[2]

Silence and the Response of Awe

Silence is at the core of Berryman's diagram (see fig. 3). The first layer of language occurs when in a moment of stillness the reality of God breaks in upon us, and we experience the presence of God. In awe we respond not in words, but with "Ahh!—Aha!—Haha!" The surprise of God's breaking in causes us to catch our breath with an "Ahh!" The "Aha!" of recognition follows when we realize it is God, and joy flows into "Haha!" at the wonder and the paradox of

Figure 3 *Layers of Religious Language*

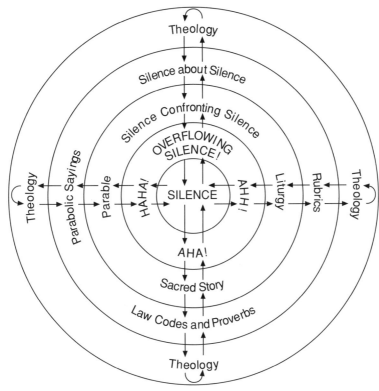

Jerome W. Berryman, *Godly Play: A Way of Religious Education* (San Francisco: HarperSanFrancisco, 1991), 152.

what is revealed of God and of ourselves in the presence of the Almighty.

The following account, written by a man of fifty-five years recalling his childhood experience, illustrates this first layer of language. As a five-year-old child watching a colony of ants at work, it dawned on him that he was gigantic in comparison to the ants, so large that he was invisible to the ants even though, at a glance, he could see their every move and could destroy them if he wished. He turned to leave the ants, and as he did he

> saw there was a tree not far away, and the sun was shining. There were clouds and blue sky that went on for ever and ever. And suddenly I was

tiny—so little and weak and insignificant that it didn't really matter at all whether I existed or not. And yet, insignificant as I was, my mind was capable of understanding that the limitless world I could see was beyond my comprehension. I could know myself to be a minute part of it all. I could understand my lack of understanding.

A watcher would have to be incredibly big to see me and the world around me as I could see the ants and their world. . . . He would have to be vaster than the world and space, and beyond understanding, and yet I *could* be aware of him—I *was* aware of him, in spite of my limitations. At the same time he was, and he was not, beyond my understanding.

The child also realized in that moment that, small as he was, he had a part to play "in the whole . . . Running indoors, delighted with my discovery, I announced happily, 'We're like ants, running about on a giant's tummy!' No one understood, but that was unimportant. I knew what I knew."[3]

Note how the first form of language is expressed in this account. In silence the boy watched the ants, and as he turned to leave, he sensed the vastness of the universe. In that moment he was aware of the presence of the Great Watcher—Ahh!—and of his own smallness. Understanding dawned—Aha!—as he became aware of the Watcher and of the paradox that at the same time he was and was not beyond his understanding. In glee—Haha!—the child announced, "We're like ants, running about on a giant's tummy!" At five the boy could not tell what he had experienced; he did not have the necessary language of words. But the encounter was real and profound.

This first layer of religious language flows from the core of religious knowledge—the experiencing of God—and is an expression of worship. Since no words are used, it is actually prelanguage—the wordless language of experience.

Liturgy, Sacred Stories, Parables

In Berryman's second layer of language, we simply participate in liturgy without theologizing. We enter the stories of Scripture and through our imaginations live them; we enter the parables and reflect on their meanings. This is a language of deep experiential involvement in the rituals and stories of our faith, which engages the affective, emotional aspects of our being as well as our thinking. As children enter the stories and experience the liturgy, they can meet God and know God in affective ways that they cannot process logically or describe in words. But in those stories, parables, and symbolic rituals, God can minister to their deep inner needs.

Berryman and others have developed an approach to religious education that largely uses this second level of religious language. An adult leader tells a parable or sacred story to a group of children using visual materials to dramatize the event. Throughout the telling of the story, the storyteller's eyes focus on the materials, drawing the children into the story also. After the telling of the story, the children may take the materials, lay out the figures, and relive the story. Children who are too young to accurately reconstruct the story in words are able to reconstruct it with the materials and meet God again.

Children may also enter Bible stories as they sit cuddled up with a parent, listening at bedtime, or as a well-prepared Sunday school teacher brings a biblical event to life through storytelling. Parents and teachers can provide the stories, rituals, and materials that give children the opportunity to participate in this second layer of language. As they enter the story or experience the liturgical symbols, we trust God to meet the children and to lead them to the discoveries and the meaning they need.

Rubric, Law Codes, Parabolic Sayings

In the third layer of religious language we begin to discuss the meaning of the liturgy, stories, and parables we have experienced. *Rubric* refers to giving directions on how to perform liturgical rituals and explaining the meaning of the rituals. We begin to analyze the sacred stories, identifying examples in the narratives that can become laws and codes to guide our lives. The meaning of a parable is probed and captured in parabolic sayings intended to sum up the parable. The third layer of language attempts to discover and communicate in abstract word symbols the meaning of liturgy, sacred stories, and parables.

In small groups and Sunday school classes when we discuss the meaning and application of biblical texts, we are using this third level of religious language. Religious traditions have laws and rules for their members, which are passed on to children and newcomers. These, too, belong in Berryman's third layer of language.

Theology

The outer layer of religious language is theology—language about God. All we have learned about God through experience and the study of Scripture is boiled down into a system of abstract words that precisely describe what God is like, how God acts in the world, who we are, and how we relate to God, others, and the world.

Each layer of religious language is more abstract than the one before it. Adults who have developed their abstract thinking abilities can move back and forth across the layers of language with ease. Too often, however, we work our way to the outer layer and, once we have learned the language of theology, are content to debate theological issues but fail to move back into the center to relive the stories and experience God anew. Without the continuing experience of God, theology becomes words about words.

Children move only as far out in the layers of language as their cognitive development allows. The abstract outer layer is meaningless to them, but they can profoundly experience the inner layers. And those inner layers provide real knowledge—a primary, foundational knowledge of God. In spite of cognitive limitations, a genuine knowing of God is open to children. Parents and teachers can have the joy of setting the stage for children to experience God in moments of silence and through liturgy, sacred stories, and parables.

Common Ground

The second layer of religious language provides a common ground where children of various ages, teenagers, and adults can meet and experience God together. The language of liturgy and story is a language we all understand in a way uniquely suited to each of us. We each enter the same story together with the intention of listening to God and of taking time to reflect on the meaning of God's story. What we hear varies depending on our level of development, particular needs, and readiness to hear, but we can all experience awe and wonder in the presence of God.

John 12:27–29 gives an example of how this works. A few days before his death, Jesus spoke about the kernel of wheat falling into the ground and dying. Then he said:

> "Now my soul is troubled. And what should I say—'Father, save me from this hour'? No, it is for this reason that I have come to this hour. Father, glorify your name." Then a voice came from heaven, "I have glorified it, and I will glorify it again." The crowd standing there heard it and said that it was thunder. Others said, "An angel has spoken to him."

Everyone present participated in the same event. Some thought the sound they heard was thunder, others thought they heard an angel, but John heard the words God spoke. They each heard what they were ready to hear, which I am sure inspired awe in all of them.

Children, teenagers, and adults—the entire faith community—need times of worshiping and learning together. Such experiences can be meaningful for all ages if we use the language of story and liturgy, trusting the Holy Spirit to speak God's word of meaning to each person in moments of quiet listening.

A PLACE TO MEET GOD

Churches offer varied settings for the spiritual nurture of children such as Sunday school, midweek clubs, choirs, children's worship, and opportunities to participate in activities of the full faith community. Maria Montessori, a European educator of an earlier generation, designed a setting for children that was "between the classroom and the church." It was a place where children came to meet God and to know the deep realities of faith—a place, not for instruction, but for experiencing the religious life.[4]

My observations suggest that few churches provide such a place for children. In the settings listed above, adults intend to supply Christian instruction, fun, and opportunities for children to build relationships in the church family, but little attention is given to worship, even in what is called children's worship. We often try to compete with the rapid paced entertainment of television, seldom giving children a quiet moment in which to meet God, and many children lose touch with the God for whom their hearts hunger.

For several years now I have worshiped with children in a quiet place where together we enter the sacred stories and parables to listen and respond to God. Our goal is not to instruct the children in worship but to set the stage for them to meet God and to worship. Our children have Sunday school and a midweek club for instruction and fun; they participate in faith community activities and choir. And they also have a quiet place where children do meet God. In the following section I invite you to come with me to children's worship and see how children use the religious language described by Berryman in a place between the classroom and the church.

Worshiping with Children

Our children worship with the whole congregation for the first part of the service each Sunday morning. Then after a few moments of conversation with the pastor, they leave the sanctuary and go to their worship areas. Two adult or teenage greeters bring the children to their worship area, and at the door they pause to help the children get ready to enter their special place of worship. As worship leader, I take my place in the worship circle before the children arrive and prepare my heart to be in God's presence. One by one the children come in and choose a seat on the floor in the worship circle. I greet and welcome each child by name, learning the names of any children who are new.

When all are seated in the circle I say, "This is a special place. It is a very special place because we have come here to be with God—to listen to God, to talk to God, and to hear the stories of God. In this place we walk more slowly and we talk more softly, because someone may be listening to God, and we don't want to disturb them. We need a way to get ready to be in this special place with God. You don't need me to tell you how to get ready; you can do it yourself, because quiet comes from the inside. Let's all close our eyes and take just a moment to relax and get quiet from the inside."

After a few quiet moments I continue, "We can't see Jesus with our eyes, can we? But in our imaginations we can see him. Do you see Jesus coming into our room? He walks over and sits down right beside you. Now is your time to tell him anything you want to tell him."

One morning during this quiet time, as I silently prayed for each child in the circle, I looked up to see who I might have missed. To my amazement, every child, with eyes tightly closed, was intently focused on this time of communion with Jesus. After a few minutes I close our time of prayer with a short expression of thanksgiving. "Thank you, Jesus, for being with us and loving us. Amen."

"We talk to God when we pray, and when we sing," I remind the children. "Let's sing our love to God, using our voices and our hands." The children love to sign the words as we sing "Oh God, We Adore You" or "God Is So Good," often ending our singing time with "Be Still and Know."

"Now we are ready to hear one of God's stories. Watch," I say, as I leave the circle, go to the story shelf, and return with a gold box. With my eyes focused on the box I am holding, I begin the story. "I wonder if this might be a parable. Parables are precious, like gold, and this box is gold." I caress the box as I would a precious object. "It looks like a present. Parables are like presents, you know. We can't buy them, or take them, or steal them. They're already ours." Setting the box on the floor in front of me I continue, "There's another reason this might be a parable." Slowly I outline the lid of the box. "It has a lid on it. Parables seem to have lids on them too. But if you can lift the lid, you discover there is something very precious inside. I know, let's look and see if there is a parable inside."

Placing the box beside me and opening the lid, I lift out a piece of green felt and begin to unfold it, spreading it on the floor in front of me. "This is so green and soft and warm. I wonder what could be so green? It might be a bush or a tree or a big green balloon. Hmmm. It might be a meadow. I wonder if there is anything else? There is this. I wonder what it could be," I ponder as I spread a light blue oval of felt on the green. "It could be a piece of the sky or water." Taking three dark blue felt pieces from the box, I continue, "These are so dark. There is hardly any light in them. I wonder what they are?"

After placing the dark blue pieces, I lay down a long narrow piece of brown felt. "This looks like a road. But there are more. If I put one here, and one here, I can make this place strong." As more strips are added, building a square, I say, "I can make this place stronger and stronger and stronger. I wonder what it is? It could be a corral or a log house. It has an inside and an outside. We need a way to go out and come in. I know. I'll make a gate." I turn back the ends of one set of strips, making a gate. "I wonder who lives here." Taking five sheep from the box, I place them in the enclosure. "Sheep. If sheep live here, it's a sheepfold. They call it a fold because the sheep are enfolded safely inside." As I speak those words my hands surround the sheepfold in a protecting gesture.

Now the setting is laid for the parable. After a pause, and with my eyes focused on the materials, the story continues. "Once there was someone who said such wonderful things and did such amazing things that the people began to follow him. But they didn't know who he was. So one day, they just had to ask him. And he said, 'I am the Good Shepherd.'" I hold up the Good Shepherd figure for the children to see and then move the figures as the story proceeds. "'I know every one of my sheep by name. My sheep know the sound of my voice so that when I call them from the fold, they follow me. I always go ahead of my sheep to show them the way. I show them the way to good, green grass. I show them the way to cool, clear, still water. And when there are places of danger, I show them the way to pass through, so that they can come safely back to the fold again.'"

With the sheep safely back in the fold again and the Good Shepherd standing close by, we pause to reflect. "I wonder if these sheep have names? I wonder if they are happy in this place? I wonder how they feel to have the Shepherd so close? I wonder if you have ever had to go through places of danger? I wonder if you ever feel the Good Shepherd near?"[5] After each question, we take time to think.

"Now, watch closely as I put the materials away," I instruct the children, making eye contact with them for the first time since the story began. "You may want to work with the materials, and you will need to know how to put them away so that they will be ready for the next person." I fold the materials carefully, replace them in the box, and carry it back to the story shelf. Then I bring the Bible to the circle and read, "Jesus said, 'I am the Good Shepherd.'"

For the response time, which follows the story, the children choose their work. One by one they choose whether to take the materials for a story and work with them, to spend time in the worship center just talking to Jesus and looking at the words of the story, which are marked in the Bible, or to make a picture of something they were thinking about while listening to the story. Adults are available to help children find the materials they need, but each child works on his or her own, processing in God's presence whatever they desire.

When parents come for the children, the children put their materials away and then receive a blessing before they leave. With my arm around the child, I say the child's name and, "I'm so glad you came to worship today. This week remember, the Good Shepherd knows your name. Go in Jesus' love."

From the time the children enter the worship area until they leave, an atmosphere of quiet is maintained. Adults and children alike use quiet voices so that no one who is talking to God will be disturbed. It is not a place for person-to-person interaction; that occurs in other settings. In worship we have come to be with God and to listen to God. When parents come for the children, they wait outside the room so that the children still working will not be disturbed.

How Children Respond

Jonathan, a third grader, was going to be in my group when we started the new children's worship. He is the boy mentioned in chapter 6 whose teenage sister, Angela, had died of cancer, and his grief had been great. As I prepared to tell the Good Shepherd parable for the children, I prayed that Jonathan would be able to meet the Good Shepherd in the parable and be comforted. For three Sundays I told the Good Shepherd story, expanding it to include the story of the lost sheep and finally of the ordinary shepherd who ran away when the wolf came. Each week Jonathan listened intently to the story, but during response time he happily made whatever his friend John was making—items that had nothing to do with the story.

On the fourth Sunday I presented the story of the Light. "Once there was someone who said such wonderful things and did such amazing things that the people began to follow him. But they didn't know who he was. So they just had to ask him, and he said, 'I am the Light.'" I lit the Christ candle, and we enjoyed the light. "Those who love the Light," I told the children, "take their light from the Light." Then I proceeded to light a small candle for each child, holding up their candle, looking them in the eyes, and saying their name, "Emily, this is your light."

It was not a good morning. Several children were distracted, making comments to get the attention of others, but I plowed ahead, saying, "See how the light has spread. So many have received their light from the Light, and yet the Light is still the same." I lit Jonathan's candle and turned to speak to him when he blurted out, "That's Angela's light." "Yes," I responded, "Angela did take her light from the Light, and now Angela is with the Light forever, and this is Jonathan's light."

At the close of the story I let Jonathan be the first to choose his work, thinking that he might want to use the materials from the story of the Light. Instead, he took the Good Shepherd parable box and spent the rest of the hour immersed in the story of the Good Shepherd. The following Sunday Jonathan again chose to work with the Good Shepherd story. One of the adult workers went over to Jonathan and began asking him questions about the story. In just a few minutes Jonathan put the materials away. Was he finished with the story, or had his time with the Good Shepherd been interrupted because he could not verbalize what he knew and felt of the Shepherd as he simply entered the story? I think the latter was true, since the next Sunday he again returned to work with the Good Shepherd. Somehow, the symbol of the Light connected with Jonathan's deep inner feelings and brought into his consciousness Angela and his grief. He now knew where to go with his pain. He went to the Good Shepherd and spent time with him in the story. Maybe someday Jonathan will be able to tell me what went on between him and the Shepherd on those three Sunday mornings, but as a third grader he could only be with the Shepherd.

Not all children encounter God so profoundly, but they do listen and watch intently as the stories are told. They enjoy working with the story materials and getting to choose what they will draw or make with the art materials. Children who have deep inner struggles, such as dealing with death, having to adjust to a new home in a new country, or the breaking up of their family, are the ones whose work reflects the deepest insight or the most time spent with the Good Shepherd. Children for whom life is safe and happy value a time and a place to be with God, and hurting children, who desperately need healing for their spirit, find healing in that time and place.

When I first observed this form of children's worship, I wondered whether or not it was constructive to force some children, especially active little boys, into this slow-moving, quiet setting. It was almost impossible for John, a fourth grader, to sit still; it seemed his body wanted to be in constant motion. When I asked him what he liked best about church, he answered, "The way you give us time to think." Even active children need and appreciate time to reflect. Our society is stimulus addicted, and children need a place where they can come off that addiction and can discover the peace of quiet.[6] It is amazing how comfortably children fit into the quiet when they have had a simple orientation on how things are done in children's worship.

PRINCIPLES BEHIND THE DESIGN

The approach to children's worship just described comes from *Young Children and Worship,* a book by Sonja Stewart and Jerome Berryman. Sofia Cavalletti, an Italian educator and Hebrew scholar, is the one, however, who developed and researched this form of religious education. Certain beliefs about children and how adults can best assist them on their spiritual journey underlie Cavalletti's way of working with children. Her insights are instructive for us as we design ministries with children.

Insights on Children

The basic premise undergirding Cavalletti's work with children is the belief that children are spiritual beings. With ease they grasp the reality of the transcendent and are even more open to God than many adults. Adele Costa Gnocchi, a colleague of Cavalletti, often commented, "God and the child get along well together." When we give children opportunity to meet God, we are not attempting to force something unnatural on them. Children are born with the potential for spiritual experience, and God is the one who stimulates the activation of that potential. We have the privilege of becoming partners with God by assisting children in finding what they long for—experience with God.[7]

A child's encounter with God is not in the control of parents or teachers. We may provide a place, stories, and materials for the children; the form of religion and the relationship with God that they observe in us may influence some of their perceptions. But their relationship with God will not be a cookie-cutter version of ours, because God initiates the experiences with the children, and they process experience and respond uniquely. Some methods and content, as we will see, have proven effective, but parents and teachers must trust God—not their methods—to bring children to an awareness of God.[8]

When Jerome Berryman served as chaplain in a children's hospital and worked with children in the local church, he discovered that children are aware of the most basic questions asked by human beings. They are aware of death, the need for meaning, the threat to their freedom, and being alone. The children cry out for help with these issues, but adults seldom notice, because children do not articulate their deep questions and hunger for God in ways adults understand. However, when adults assume children may be dealing with some of these issues and give them opportunities to meet God in stories and rituals that relate to basic life issues, response indicates the importance of the issues to the children. An encounter with God seems to satisfy the whole child to the depth of his or her being, and children demonstrate joy, peace, and a beautiful calm.[9]

To say that children are spiritual beings does not assume that they are ready for spiritual disciplines or that they can be expected to consider what pleases God in all their interactions. Often children experience God in fleeting moments of awareness and may not be fully conscious of the encounter. Such glimpses of God, however, are real, and the joy, peace, and insight of those glimpses germinate within the child and someday may come into the full bloom of conscious love for God.[10]

Maria Montessori, whose understanding of children and whose approach to instruction profoundly influenced Cavalletti, identified what she called sensitive periods in the lives of children. These sensitive periods are times when children are most open to learn certain things. It is as if a drive within moves children to learn all they can about a certain topic or to master a particular skill. There is a best time for learning to talk or walk and for learning about God's love or moral responsibility. When working with children, their response indicates whether what we are trying to teach is in harmony with their present sensitivity. If they are ready for the particular learning, they will take an interest in it, be curious about the subject, and be full of questions. There will be a sense of wonder at what they discover. Repeatedly they will choose to work with materials that help them explore the topic, and as they work they will reflect joy and peace.[11]

In regard to religious education, Montessori discovered in children a sensitivity to three different themes: protection, the moral, and heroism. Early childhood is the period of sensitivity toward protection—God's protection. During later childhood a moral sensitivity surfaces, and adolescents are sensitive to heroism. When working with the Good Shepherd parable, young children focus on the fold and the protecting love of the shepherd. Older children, as they reflect on the lost sheep and the shepherd's seeking love, discover that God's protecting love also forgives when they have done wrong. Preadolescents admire the Shepherd who always walks ahead of the sheep, showing them the way through difficulties to abundant life. They want to follow Jesus into that abundant life and to be like Jesus.

At various ages children become aware of different realities of the gospel. There will never be a time in life when the person can grasp the truth as easily as in the sensitive period. Realities comprehended during these prime times for learning live on within, sustaining us. If the sensitive period passes and the child has not made the critical discoveries, the need for that knowing remains as an inner "unappeased hunger."[12]

Christian parents and teachers are often deeply concerned about the moral education of their children. Cavalletti cautions that to emphasize moral education too early may actually distort a child's morality. Early childhood is a time for being loved and protected by God, for enjoying God's love and responding in love. This love relationship is the firm foundation on which to build the moral life. Emphasizing what young children must do to please God may cause them to focus on what they must do to earn God's love and pleasure. A strained, often fearful relationship with God may develop as the child feels the pressure of *doing* to please God. Cavalletti cautions:

> There is a "time for everything," as Ecclesiastes says, and early childhood is not the time for moral effort . . . we must not anticipate and confuse the times. If we do, we preclude the child's access to that aspect of God the child most needs. In our estimation, we compromise the child's very moral formation, which should be based on love, and should be the response of the child's love to the love that God first gave him [or her].[13]

This does not mean that young children are never required to live within reasonable behavioral expectations. Earlier we discussed the importance of such boundaries. It does mean, however, that in correcting children who have not behaved appropriately, we do not bring God's displeasure into the conversation to pressure the child into conformity. In our times of structured instruction with young children we should focus on God's love and protection, not on God's demands and judgment. Such a perspective does not devalue the moral life, but rather, "we believe that the more profound, deeply felt, and enjoyed the child's religious experience is, the more ready, autonomous, and genuine will be the response of the older child."[14] We want our children to obey God because they do not want to cause grief to the one who loves them. As they become aware of their moral failures, we also want them to discover that their loving God forgives and wants to help children to do the right thing. The importance of the initial love relationship with God cannot be overemphasized; everything else in spiritual formation builds on it in the proper time.

Cavalletti found that children who experienced very little human love were some of the happiest when working with the Good Shepherd parable. As they encountered the Good Shepherd, they could sense the love of Jesus even though they had not experienced good human models of love from which to build an understanding of God's love. Children dealing with illness and other major traumas also found special comfort in the Good Shepherd.[15] Through stories, especially the parable of the Good Shepherd, we can set the stage for children, even the most vulnerable, to experience God's love.

Insights on Method

How can parents and teachers open the way for children to experience God? What is our role? Children need to receive from us the proclamation of the gospel, the good news about God's love expressed through Jesus. This proclamation is given to the children through the stories of Scripture. Dorothy Sayers called the Bible "God's autobiography,"[16] and it is the best source for getting to know the author, God. As you noticed in the account of our children's worship, a unique way of proclaiming the Good News to children was used. We will now look in more detail at the concepts behind those methods.

Adults must provide a community in which children can hear the Word and can meet God. Children need a sense of belonging in the larger faith community and in their worship setting. These special worship groups will be more truly a community when the participating adults see themselves as learners and worshipers along with the children. We too need to hear the Good News anew and to probe its meaning more deeply. Even as we tell the stories, we must listen for God's word to us. Children can be encouraged to enter the stories, reflect on their meaning, and respond in worship when the adults in their community model those behaviors.[17]

Montessori and Cavalletti found that children experienced God more meaningfully when adults created a special place in which children could worship in ways appropriate to their particular sensitivities and needs. It is important for children to sense that they belong to the faith community as a whole, but they also need their special place of worship—a place where they can reflect on the gospel themes that are critical to their spiritual development and, through working with stories and liturgical symbols, can discover meaning for the rituals of their church. If children do not have such a place where they "can come in touch with the religious reality in a way and at a rhythm suitable to children, there is the danger the child will pass by great things without ever being able to grasp, internalize and make these realities [their] own."[18]

At the close of Sunday school each week, our children's worship leaders transform the Sunday school classroom into a place for worship. All the chairs are removed, art materials are arranged on a large table, and a small worship table is set up with a Bible and a picture of Jesus and children. Open shelves that contain materials for each of the stories the children have heard in worship are rolled to the front of the room. Even though some of the children come to this same physical space for choir practice or Sunday school, these simple alterations transform it into a place of worship.

Proclaiming the Good News to children in a special place of worship involves words. Words are wonderful tools of communication and the cause of much miscommunication. Montessori cautioned that in the religious instruction of children our words should be few and weighty.[19] The words used in telling stories should be carefully chosen to simply and briefly, in narrative form, lay out the great truths of the gospel for the children. In the Good Shepherd parable presented earlier, you probably noted that no amplification or explanations were added to the story. It basically gave the words of Scripture to the children. The language of story communicates with young children and with adults, but when we try to talk about the meaning of the story and explain to children what they should be hearing from the story, then miscommunication begins to occur.[20]

Jesus said,

> When the Spirit of truth comes, he will guide you into all the truth; for he will not speak on his own, but will speak whatever he hears, and he will declare to you the things that are to come. He will glorify me, because he will take what is mine and declare it to you.
>
> John 16:13–14

Do we believe that the Spirit of truth, who has come, guides children into truth as well as adults? The method of introducing children to the gospel that we are discussing here is based on the belief that God's Spirit does lead children to the truth they need. Our part, as adults worshiping with children, is to provide children a setting and in few words give them one of God's stories. We then get out of the way so that the Spirit of truth can lead the children to meet God in the story and to discover precious realities suited for them. The Spirit of God knows the mind and heart of the child and how best to communicate. We must never forget that we are merely assistant teachers or worship leaders, but God does give us the privilege of assisting, and he honors us by sometimes speaking through us to the children.[21]

Jerome Berryman calls entering biblical stories with children "godly play." Play is the child's work. Godly play is working with God's stories and liturgy in a way that is appropriate for children, in a playful manner. For children to engage in godly play, the language of the Christian faith, the stories, and the symbols are made into objects that children can manipulate.[22] The green pastures and still waters of the shepherd's psalm become pieces of felt the children can handle and feel. They move pictures of the Good Shepherd and the sheep through the green pastures, by the still waters, through the places of danger, and safely back to the fold again. A beautiful gold box holds the materials and makes concrete the precious nature of the parable. Simple wooden figures are used to enact the events of Scripture such as Abram and Sarai making their way across the desert in response to the God who promised to show them the way, or Mary and Joseph on the way to Jerusalem.

As they work with the materials, children grasp with their hands the stories and ideas of Scripture and through this means are able to grasp them with their hearts. Through manipulating the materials, children are able to do in a sensorimotor form what they are not yet able to do in abstract thought. They work with theological concepts and discover the connection between biblical stories and their lives. In the process of handling the materials, reliving the stories, and drawing pictures of their impressions from the story, they discover meanings and grow in their understanding of God.[23] These meanings and understandings are not within the child's grasp through abstract symbols of words but through sensorimotor experience and living the stories through their imaginations.

The goal of godly play is not to give children prepackaged answers but to teach them how to enter God's stories to find the answers that give meaning and direction in their young lives. Children learn to enter stories as they watch adults enter them, with feeling, concentrated reflection, and respect. They learn the method more fully through the experience of working with the materials and modeling the teacher's use of them. By teaching a method of entering Scripture rather than concentrating on teaching specific answers, we demonstrate respect for each child's ability to hear God speak and our faith in God to communicate with children.[24]

Another goal of godly play is to stimulate a sense of wonder and mystery in children as they approach the stories. Again, our actions during the storytelling communicate wonder and mystery to children. We model wonder only when we have spent enough time in the story to be moved by its reality ourselves. Wonder is an important magnet that can draw children to Scripture. Cavalletti states, "Wonder . . . attracts us with irresistible force toward the object of our astonishment." It draws us to become "immersed in the contemplation of something that exceeds us."[25] Wondering takes time and a worthy object. In our fast-moving, noise-cluttered society, children are seldom given time to wonder and may be deprived of God's deep truths as we try to keep them entertained. Children need a place where they have time to wonder about the mystery of the gospel.

Approaching Scripture with a sense of wonder and mystery gives children an open rather than a closed view of the Bible. They are drawn to discover what they can from God's stories now, knowing intuitively that there is always more to be discovered later. This attitude sets the stage for a lifelong exploration of Scripture, rather than the collection of "right" facts and answers boxed by the child's concrete mind, later to be thrown away because they proved inadequate.

Let children have the joy of discovery by inviting them to enter stories and giving them the time to make their own discoveries. In godly play, several "I wonder" questions follow the story. They point children toward possible discoveries but do not give answers. When ready, children will joyfully make their discoveries. It may be this week or next, one year from now or two. From time to time adults may share one of their discoveries to let children see their joy and that they are still finding new treasures in the Bible, not to make sure the children get that point.[26]

Following the presentation of the story, children are given time to work with story or art materials. The term *work* is used for two reasons. First, it refers to play that probes the mystery of great realities, and second, it gives to what the children are doing the value our society places on work. What the children do is significant.

In this time of quiet work, children reconstruct the story for themselves or draw their thoughts, and as they do they have opportunity for conversation with the inner Teacher. It is the time when they personalize the story to their lives. It is a time of intimate, firsthand experience with God, which the adult cannot and should not enter unless invited by the child. To burst in at our initiative is to interfere with the inner Teacher's work.[27]

This does not mean adults should never discuss with children the meaning of the stories they explore. Berryman's third layer of language—rubric, law codes, and parabolic sayings—calls for talking about meanings. There is a place for discussing with older children what they see in biblical events and how the meanings apply to them. When time allows, teachers, parents, and children alike profit from engaging children in conversation about their artwork. But the focus of godly play and children's worship is on letting the inner Teacher speak to each child.

Material for all the stories told to date in the present church year should be available to the children. It is important that they have the opportunity to return to a story as often as they desire.[28] The first Sunday Leighann heard the Good Shepherd parable, she chose to go to the worship center; there she found the words of the story in the Bible. Then she took a piece of paper, drew an open Bible, and began to copy the words about the Good Shepherd. Her parents came for her before she had finished, but the next Sunday she took her picture from her folder and finished copying the story. After being absent for a few Sundays with a broken arm, she returned and heard the story of Noah. For her work she created out of modeling clay a detailed biblical character complete with headdress and staff. When I mentioned to her mother that Leighann had made a masterful Noah, she responded, "Oh yes. Leighann told me she had made the Shepherd." A few weeks later at an open house I watched as Leighann took the Good Shepherd parable box from the shelf and told the story to her family.

When I told a friend about Leighann, she commented, "The child must be very insecure." My immediate thought was, "Oh, no," and then I saw the whole picture. Leighann belonged to a military family; they were in Toronto for just one year. The first Sunday the family attended church they announced, "We'll be worshiping with you all year. What can we do? We want to be involved." With that attitude I assumed this family had mastered the art of living a healthy though very mobile life, and I never gave a second thought to how an eight-year-old feels about being uprooted again and again. How fortunate that she could return to the secure comfort of time with the Shepherd as often as she needed to.

Children should be allowed to work only with materials for the stories they have heard. If they use the wooden figures for creative play, they are not entering the Bible story to work with it.[29] Dramatic play through which their imaginations freely create the story line is an important part of a child's life, but it is not the purpose of godly play.

As I talk about being quiet and taking time for wondering, you may be asking, is it possible to get stimulus-addicted children to be quiet and take time to wonder? Not by simply saying, "Okay, children; now we're going to be quiet and wonder." Children can enjoy the wondering stillness, however, if we prepare them for it. I tell children I have discovered they can do things very well if adults just take the time to show them how. We then show them how to walk more slowly and talk more softly, how to get their art materials and work with the stories. We walk them through each of the expectations of the structure of our time together, and they learn the structure well. When a child forgets, we go to him or her and quietly say, "Remember, in this special place we talk more softly, and we do our own work because someone may be talking to God, and we don't want to disturb them." Remembering this is important for adults as well.

Insights on Content

A method is effective only if it deals with sound and worthy content. Cavalletti and Berryman offer interesting insights into the religious content most appropriate for children.

Repeatedly we have stated that our goal is to set the stage for children to encounter God. Christians believe Jesus Christ was God in human form and is our most complete revelation of God. It therefore seems appropriate that children in a Christian church should be introduced to God through Jesus Christ. Godly play, then, is Christ centered. Children meet Jesus before being introduced to the historical events that show God working with the people of God. Although through godly play children learn about key events in Jesus' life, the major emphasis is on a relationship with Jesus and with the mystery of his life. Children first get to know and love Jesus in the parable of the Good Shepherd. How can they help but love the one who knows them by name, leads them through danger to safety, seeks them when they are lost, and protects them from the attacking wolf? A relationship with Jesus the Good Shepherd can be established in early childhood and can grow for a lifetime.[30]

In children's worship during Advent and Lent, we get ready to celebrate "the mystery of Christmas, the mystery of Easter." Can children grasp the full meaning of Christ's coming, death, and resurrection? Can we as adults? No, but awareness of the mystery draws us to explore, wonder, and discover more and more, year after year.

Cavalletti believes "it is the greatest realities that are to be given to the youngest children," and "the nucleus of the Christian mystery in its greatest content" is in parables. In addition to the parable of the

Good Shepherd, Cavalletti recommends that we lead children to explore the mystery of the kingdom of God through the kingdom parables. For years religious educators have warned that parables are materials unfit for children; far too abstract for them to grasp. But Cavalletti claims that parables "will gradually unfold all [their] riches to the child" in a way that offers an ever widening and complete vision of God and God's kingdom. This unfolding process makes it possible for persons never to have to "disown anything received previously."[31]

Another reason for the importance of parables is that they engage children affectively.[32] Children seem able to process deep realities at an affective level sometime before they can conceptualize the truths. To give the great realities of the faith to children, those realities must be in story form. Great theological themes can be woven through sacred stories as well as parables—themes such as the reality of a God who speaks, guides, protects, forgives, and faithfully keeps promises.

Godly play, when used with children in worship, is structured to follow the order of worship observed by the child's faith community. The children prepare to be in God's presence, express their adoration in prayer and song, hear the proclamation of God's Word in the story, have opportunity to respond to God, and leave with a blessing. In churches that observe Holy Communion weekly, children participate in a feast each time they meet. Children are being grounded in their religious traditions through these experiences. Berryman believes children need such grounding.[33] Many adults have little understanding of worship and have never been instructed in their religious traditions. As they participate in godly play with the children, they too receive significant grounding in their faith tradition.

Repeatedly throughout this book we have emphasized the importance of children participating with adults in the rituals of their faith. The most important ritual in most Christian traditions is Holy Communion. Through godly play children can discover deep meaning in communion. During the Lenten season they can go with Jesus and the disciples to the upper room for the Last Supper. They can see the bread held high, broken, and given to the disciples; they can see the cup held high and hear the words of Jesus. The storyteller will ask, "Have you ever been close to this table? Have you ever heard the words of Jesus?" A few weeks later the children will listen and watch as the Good Shepherd leads the sheep to the communion table to feed them, and the children will discover that the Shepherd invites us to that table also to feed us. At the end of the story we reflect, "I wonder if you have ever been close to this table? I wonder if you have ever felt the Good Shepherd near in this place?" Such godly play can open the great Christian tradition of Holy Communion to children for meaningful participation.[34]

In our discussion of godly play, you may have noted the absence of comments on adults building relationships with the children. Although we enjoy worshiping with our friends, the purpose of worship is for communion with God, and that is the focus of godly play. However, deep bonds often form between adults and children who experience genuine worship together week after week.[35]

APPLICATION

You may be wondering, given the realities of your Christian education ministries, what you can do with the ideas of this chapter. One option would be to fully implement the principles by structuring your children's worship for godly play.[36] The approach works best with a group of fifteen to twenty children and three adults. Some churches have two or more groups for different age levels. Large churches may feel they are not able to offer godly play for all their children, but it can be an option for those who desire it. One church invited parents to bring their preschool children to worship on Thursday mornings; another offered twelve weeks of Saturday worship times. Selected Sunday school classes can also use the approach. Another large church used the stories from *Young Children and Worship* with a small group of families for a time of intergenerational biblical reflection and worship.

Another option is to build some of the principles from this chapter into the ministries already in place in your church. Evaluate what you currently offer to children and identify how ministries could incorporate elements from the chapter so that your children will have enhanced opportunities for knowing God.

Nine

PILGRIMS TOGETHER ON THE JOURNEY

Three-year-old Paul stood in front of us, makeshift pack on his back, a length of rope attached to his shoulder strap, and a walking stick in hand. "I'm going hitchhiking," he announced. As his parents and I chuckled over the misuse of terms and as we sensed his excitement, little did we realize where that love for hiking would lead him. Since that day, when I took his picture standing on a pile of sand by the lake, he has hiked the path through the pasture beside Grandpa's house, the trail to the top of Natural Bridge, the Canadian and Colorado Rockies, to the peaks of twenty-seven mountains in Taiwan—all over ten thousand feet high he tells me—and along the trails of Kentucky's Red River Gorge. I am thankful that on many of those excursions he had companions suited to the challenges of the trail, but I am also grateful that I have walked some of those paths with him.

THE METAPHOR: WALKING AS PILGRIMS ON A JOURNEY

One of the most common biblical metaphors for living is walking. When God came to make a covenant with Abram, God commanded him to "walk before me, and be blameless" (Gen. 17:1). Throughout Deuteronomy, Moses instructed the people to walk in God's ways (Deut. 10:12; 13:5; 26:17; 28:9). To those who would follow his statutes, God gave a wonderful promise: "I will walk among you, and will be your God, and you shall be my people" (Lev. 26:12). The metaphor appears repeatedly in the Psalms and in Isaiah. The psalmist spoke of people walking in the light of God's countenance (Ps. 89:15), and Isaiah called the people to "walk in the light of the LORD" (Isa. 2:5). In the New Testament the apostles Paul and John picked up the theme of the walk. John invites his readers to walk in the light as Jesus himself is in the light, enjoy fellowship with one another, and experience the blood of Jesus cleansing them from all sin (1 John 1:7). When we live our lives according to God's design, we are not alone on the path; we experience the warmth, illumination, and transformation of God's presence and the encouragement, support, and joy of fellowship with other travelers—pilgrims.

Exodus is the story of a journey—the journey of God's people out of slavery, through the wilderness, and into the Promised Land. The Israelites walked, old and young together, learning along the way. Through experience they learned what great things God could do and that God heard their prayers and granted their desires even when expressed as complaints. They also discovered the consequences of refusing to trust God. On the journey they became a people, a nation, instead of a group of freed slaves as they had been at the start. Christians often see the Exodus as a metaphor of their spiritual journey. Release from sin that had enslaved them leads them into a lifelong journey with God, a journey of learning and becoming. We do not take that journey alone; we, too, make our pilgrimage with God's people, walking with young and old, family and friends, those we like, and those who stretch us.

The metaphor for education preferred by noted educator Ted Ward is that of a life-walk to be shared. When we go for a walk, we have a purpose and a destination, but our purpose is not just to get to the destination; the "experiences of going there are as important as the arrival."[1] Although many persons may walk with a similar purpose, their experiences will vary depending on who walks with them, the time of day or year, and what they are tuned in to see or hear. Education and spiritual formation should be purposeful but are not predictable. Ward also suggests that Christians must be alert to the needs of those along the path of life and must reach out to help meet their needs.

After years of listening to children talk about life, including their spiritual life, Jane and Robert Coles[2] described children as young pilgrims. As the children traveled the ordinary days of life, from time to time they sensed a spiritual purpose. Like adults, periodically they stopped the business of doing to wonder about the meaning of their past and about what God planned for them in the future. They looked back over the section of life's journey they had completed and looked forward to the destination of their path.

The spiritual journey is not a path separate from the rest of life, walked by one's spirit. It is the path of everyday living where God meets and walks with us, where we respond to God with our whole developing self. The journey begins at conception and continues until we no longer walk this earth. Every portion of the journey is important because what we learn and who we become along each section of the way influences what we see, hear, and become in the future. Those who walk with us also contribute to how we experience the journey.

In the earlier chapters of this book as we traced the developmental journey of children, two themes surfaced repeatedly: the need for community and the importance of story. These elements are essential to the spiritual development not only of children but teenagers and adults as well. When young and old in the community of faith—the family of God—journey together in commitment to one another led by God, beautiful, enriching spiritual formation occurs for all. When children are included as respected, active participants in the community of faith, they draw us all back into the story of our faith and help us reactivate our imaginations to experience the story anew. This chapter will explore the importance and the mutual benefit of the family of God journeying together in community, learning the master story, and seeing God in the lives and through the eyes of others.

Dangers along the Way

Although hiking alone in the wilderness may be prescribed as a means for deep reflection and self-discovery, at some critical point in life, hiking is most enjoyable when shared with others. Not only is the shared journey more fun, it is also safer. The more dangerous the terrain, the more important the presence of wise, skilled companions. My nephew Paul did not climb the Taiwanese mountains alone but with friends who could encourage one another along the steep path, together enjoy the view and the glory of reaching the top, and give first aid or go for help if needed.

Danger lurks along the paths walked by our children and their parents. If they are to safely negotiate the journey with increasing strength and sensitivity and without suffering debilitating wounds, then wise, committed companions must join them on the way. Teenagers, young adults, persons in midlife, and seniors all need companions from the faith community on their life-walk. The church faces the challenge of being a community of pilgrims on the way together, inviting others to leave their aimless wandering and join them on the journey. The church has a greater potential than any other institution for providing the community so desperately needed by persons of all ages; it is the means God designed to provide support and resources for life's journey.

Our world is not a safe place. The news media report ethnic cleansing and guerilla warfare; violence breaks out in schools and on the streets of our cities; divorce and abuse are common in all communities. Some young couples wonder whether to have a family. Do they want to bring children into the world to face such dangers? The risks are high, especially if the family tries to walk alone.

Dangers in Families

Because of the mobility in societies at the end of the twentieth century, many families find themselves separated from their normal support systems or from key family members. Probably the most drastic version of this separation exists in parts of the world where families experiencing poverty with no hope of adequate income close to home decide that it is necessary for one parent to leave the country, find work, and send money home to support the family. One current example of this phenomenon is the hundreds of Filipino wives and mothers working in Hong Kong to make the money needed by their families at home in the Philippines. Although the extended family cares for the children, they are deprived of enjoying their mother's love.

The working parent experiences great sacrifice and dreadful loneliness. How they need the family of God in the new land.

Even in North America most nuclear families live at a distance from aunts, uncles, cousins, and grandparents. Both father and mother in many of these families work outside the home and return to the family with depleted energy and emotional resources after the stress of the day. As we have seen, God did not intend for a father and a mother to shoulder the full load of child rearing without the support of an extended family and a faith community. Will our faith communities connect with young people and become an extended family for them?

In chapter 3 we noted that many young parents today come from broken homes and have had only small pieces of quality time with their parents. They did not learn how to parent by seeing others care wisely and lovingly for children and, consequently, they face the responsibilities of parenting without adequate skills. Also, many young adults bring to their marriage and new home the brokenness of generational sins such as abuse and addiction. Without healing and restoration, they will pass their brokenness on to the next generation. Researchers project that 40 percent of North American children in the nineties will experience the divorce of their parents, and still others will suffer from the stresses caused by a tense and troubled relationship between parents who choose to stay together.[3] The journey of many families today is rocky, with great likelihood for acquiring deep painful wounds along the way. Sadly, this is true for many families in the church as well as for those not related to the church.[4]

Dangers in the Culture

Contemporary North American culture is adrift with many people having abandoned once-shared values for a philosophy of relativism. In the past some form of the Judeo-Christian master story was the worldview through which most Americans looked at life and established their values. But in a relativistic society, all master stories are equally acceptable except for those that, like the Judeo-Christian story, make exclusive claims. Without a shared master story and a strong commitment to the values that flow from that story, a society lacks the inner desire and strength to protect what people value. Christians can no longer expect societal reinforcement for their values.

The most powerful influence in our culture is television. On the average Americans watch twenty-six hours of television per week. By the time teenagers graduate from high school, most of them will have spent more time in front of the television than in the classroom.[5] While engrossed in television, children are not exploring, using their imagination, or building relationships; instead, they sit passively receiving the messages and values delivered by the media. The hours spent in watching television greatly exceed the hours invested at church with the faith community or in reading stories of the faith together as a family in the home. In most homes the television has a greater opportunity than does the faith community to shape the master story and values of the family.

Television communicates its story and values not only through its content but also by its form, and many of these powerfully and subtly communicated values are in opposition to Christian values. Television lulls us into the role of passive observer, whereas in the Bible we hear Jesus calling, "Come, follow me and make a difference in the world" (see Matt. 4:19). Television keeps children from actively exploring the wonders of God's creation and using their God-given creativity.

Television also creates an attitude of impatience. Commercials are designed to make us want whatever is advertised and to want it now. One commercial after another, day after day causes an inner voice to cry, "I want, I want, I want," without focusing on what is wanted. This pervasive, unfocused wanting breeds discontent, whereas Scripture calls Christians to be content (Phil. 4:11–12). Hour after hour in television stories, problems develop and are solved within a sixty-minute program leading us to believe in the quick fix. Impatiently, we try one promised solution after another for real-life problems, never taking time to discover what has gone wrong or to work through the challenges and to grow in the process. The picture on the television screen changes every nine seconds, on MTV and Sesame Street every four seconds. Extended exposure to this constant change shortens the attention span of children, teenagers, and adults—causing many to fail to discover the fascination of anything that is not in constant motion.

Thrills and fun are the ultimate values portrayed on television, whereas the Bible offers joy and happiness (John 15:11). Fun is short-lived, requiring evermore exciting thrills to recreate it. An obsession with fun leads to self-centeredness. Joy, on the other hand, is a by-product of relationships with God and others, of learning, mastering new skills, serving, and growing.

To let the television run uncontrolled is to let the media give us an anti-Christian master story and shape our worldview and that of our children. If families are to develop Christian values, television viewing must be limited, and time must be invested in relating with one another and exploring faith stories. Michael Medved, a movie critic and an orthodox Jew, has a television-free home. His family enjoys watching five hours of videos each week, and in the process of coming to an agreement on what they will watch, the children are developing excellent negotiating skills. Such a radical solution may not be right for every home, but all Christian parents must acknowledge the challenge of television and find some way to bridle it and control its influence on their values and those of their children.

Children in Crisis

In the late 1700s, the children of England's poor were in crisis. Six days a week, twelve hours a day, they worked in the mines and the factories with no opportunity for education. On Sundays they ran wild in the streets. Deep concern gripped a man by the name of Robert Raikes. What could the future hold for these children, and what would England's future be when thousands of its citizens had no education or moral training? Rakes did something about his concern. He began offering classes on Sunday where children learned to read the Bible and other stories that communicated moral truth. The Sunday school was born in response to children in crisis.

Today millions of the world's children are in crisis. Relief agencies are discovering that millions of children live on the street or work long hours to help support their families. Millions have been abducted, sold, or tricked into sexual exploitation in the brothels of large cities. A high number of these children contract AIDS, and many of the world's young AIDS victims die alone in terrible conditions because their caregivers fear contracting the disease from them.

It is estimated that in recent years one in every two hundred children worldwide has been traumatized by war. In the decade between 1985 and 1995, two million children were killed in wars, five million physically disabled, and twelve million left homeless. Thousands have been forced to take up arms and kill.

Will Christians hear the cries of these children? Will we find ways to respond? Alone, we can do very little, but we can join with others to become a voice and helping hands on behalf of the world's hurting children.[6]

Many Christians provide financial support for those on the other side of the world who serve children in crisis as the tangible presence of Christ and Christian love walking with them. But all of our communities have children in crisis who need us to walk with them.

Each day after school thousands of Canadian and American children come home to an empty apartment or house. In some situations parents could choose to be home with their child, but in most cases the children are home alone because the family needs the parents' income and there is not enough money to pay for quality day care. These latchkey children are vulnerable to anxieties, fears, and even abuse. Churches can provide after-school programs in which caring adults can meet the children, give them a snack, listen to them, help them to do homework, and involve them in activities while they wait for their parents. Some parents may be able to pay for their child to participate in an after-school program, but others will need a partial or full scholarship for their child. Retired adults can find a meaningful ministry in being present with the children, chatting with them, listening, playing table games, or reading together—just being grandparents. Genuine care for children on the part of the church may also open the door for walking with and supporting their parents.

Another crisis children face is the dreadful reality of child abuse in contemporary society. In the church we want to assume that children with whom we minister are safe from such trauma, but sadly, too often that is not the case. Those working with children in the church must be alert and responsive to evidence of child abuse. Out of love for the children, suspected abuse must be investigated and the children protected.[7] Because of concern for the whole family, the church could also provide a parents anonymous group for parents who are abusive or who fear they may become violent with their children. Often abusive parents had been abused as children and need help and support to break the abuse cycle.

Because of the brokenness of our world, care must be taken in staffing the church's children's ministries. Some churches now have teams of two working with each group of children, have application forms on which potential volunteer staff members indicate whether they have ever been convicted of abuse, and/or do not assign people to work with children until they have been in the church for one or two years and are well known. Such policies need to be presented as an expression of the church's concern for children and their safety.

When a home is broken by death or divorce, children need pastoral care and the special support of caring Christians, but in these times of crisis, children are often overlooked. We assume they are flexible and will get over the trauma in time. Often we do not realize how deeply the children are hurting, because they do not express their pain as adults do. Instead, they act out their grief, and we communicate to them additional rejection as we try to control their negative behavior. Some churches regularly organize groups to help children dealing with divorce. Hospice workers can be an excellent source of insight when we are called to walk with a grieving child. When children walk through crises, wise, competent, loving companions can make the journey more bearable and may significantly alter how a child comes through the crisis.

Support and Resources for the Journey

Ralph was an outdoorsman. For several years he joined a trail-camping class to backpack with teens in the Red River Gorge. The summer I hiked with the group, it was Ralph who loaned us his three-gallon canvas water bag so that our trail family could shower at the end of a long, hot, muddy day of backpacking. All eight of us showered from that bag, with water left over—we conserved! In his pack Ralph carried a one-burner stove on which he brewed sassafras tea and shared it with those willing to try some. He was well equipped and loved camping.

Ralph was also my handyman. When I wanted a large garden turned into lawn, Ralph did the seeding, and he came with his power saw to cut broken limbs from my trees after storms. Whenever I need something repaired, his name still comes to mind, but Ralph's life has changed. While in graduate school he did roofing during summer vacations to support his young family. In the summer of 1994, as he threw a shovelful of old shingles from a roof, his foot slipped and he fell to a concrete patio two stories below, landing on his head. Ralph never lost consciousness, but crushed vertebrae in his neck left him paralyzed.

Members of the faith community immediately rallied around Ralph, his wife Grace, and their daughters. Those who learned of the accident prayed earnestly for the family and for Ralph's healing. Friends cared for the girls, allowing Grace to stay with Ralph. In response to the anxiety generated by suddenly being unable to do anything for himself, friends volunteered to sit with Ralph around the clock, providing him with the security of knowing that someone would always be there if he should get into difficulty. Over the next months, with the help of others, Ralph worked arduously on rehabilitation and learned to operate an electric wheelchair. In the early days of being able to get around on his own again, I remember meeting him in the bookstore and watching him sign for his purchase using a tool strapped to his hand that held the pen. I rejoiced to see his progress.

Ralph, Grace, Laurel, and Annie all struggled to adjust to the drastic changes in their lives. It was far from easy, even with many supportive friends. They dreaded the first anniversary of the accident. How would they make it through the memories of that day? "Why not throw a party?" suggested their friend Pat. "We'll all come together and celebrate the good things God has done since the accident." And that is what they did. Their faith community gathered in the park, thankful that Ralph sat with them, mentally sound and able to speak in a strong voice as he told of the doctor's encouraging report earlier that day. All of us realized that even though Ralph was not walking around, God had done good things; we had seen God working in our midst. A few weeks later Ralph spoke in church, honestly sharing what he had learned in this experience and where he and the family still struggled. He helped his listeners to see their actions and their discomfort with the situation from the perspective of the person in the wheelchair. Through Ralph's patience with us, many are learning to relate more naturally with persons who face physical challenges.

As it became evident that Ralph would not experience an instantaneous, complete healing, friends realized the need for a house—built to provide as much independence as possible for someone in a wheelchair. Those friends called on the faith community to contribute funds and labor for building that house. I first visited Ralph, Grace, and the girls in their new home at the beginning of the Advent season. I dropped by to give the girls an Advent calendar to help them get ready for Christmas, and I stayed for a pleasant hour with the family. The house was a joy to see with its wide halls, beautiful oak floors, and unique stone fireplace. As we sipped tea together, Ralph and Grace reminisced about a day spent on Mount Rainier, and I enjoyed their memories with them. Both Laurel and Annie came at different times to cuddle up and give me the special gift of a little girl's love. In that hour I received so much more than the value of the three-dollar Advent calendar I had brought. They welcomed me into their family, and I left carrying with me the warmth of their peace and love, anticipating more hugs from Laurel and Annie when I meet them at church from time to time.

The Blessing of Community

As I reflect on the story of Ralph's accident, I realize anew how important community is to children whose journey leads through difficult times, the crucial role played by the faith community in support and spiritual formation of adults faced with what could be devastating realities, and what a formative blessing it is to be part of that community. Laurel and Annie have a beautiful home and parents who are putting together a new life characterized by faith and not bitterness, at least in part because the faith community has been there for them and with them through the very dark parts of their journey. The community was able to do for Ralph and his family what no handful of caring individuals could have done on their own, and no one who participated remained the same. By working together the community could be there for the long haul, long enough to discover new dimensions of God's faithfulness and unfailing love, to experience the unity and effectiveness of Christ's body, and to rejoice in the fruit of their labors.

Laurel's drawings chronicled her journey, the view from the path she walked, and the formation she experienced along the way. Shortly after the accident she held up a picture for Ralph to see. "That's you, Daddy," she said. A face with a straight line for a mouth filled the page; Daddy for her was now the face that could respond to her and speak words of love and instruction. One spring Sunday a year and a half later, Laurel presented another picture to Ralph in which bright flowers covered the page and a person wearing a smile danced among them. "That's you, Daddy," she announced again. Laurel could see and sense the spirit of her daddy dancing for joy at the beauty of God's world even though his body could not join in the dance. Within this five-year-old pilgrim had formed the ability to see an inner reality missed by many adults—a reality that brought joy.

The need for and values of community become most obvious in crisis situations, but participation in community is essential to the healthy formation of all persons in every period of life. Awareness of developmental differences has led the church to organize most of its ministries for particular age groups, even subdividing children, youth, and adults into more age-specific groupings. Although age-appropriate ministries are valuable, they are not sufficient; intergenerational community activities are also needed. In a small church that functions like a family, most activities other than the Sunday school class are intergenerational. But as a church increases in size, the generations grow apart, and soon they do not know each other or sense that they are valued by those outside their age group. In the midsize or larger church, intergenerational community is not automatic for most people; it must be created intentionally by planning intergenerational connections and activities into the life of the church.

Intergenerational Experiences

As a child I looked forward to two intergenerational church events every year. In early summer our whole church family spent a Saturday afternoon playing together at the Sunday school picnic. Senior adults who could no longer run races sat in their lawn chairs and watched us compete in creative games. Our parents and the parents of our friends set work aside and just enjoyed the fun of doing ridiculous things together. Then there was the Christmas program, which involved all ages. Together we practiced and prepared for the night when with great excitement we would retell the Christmas story. These were highlights of our family traditions in the faith community. These particular activities may not fit the interests of your church, but intergenerational traditions of some sort enrich every faith community, providing for shared joy, excitement, and the warm glow of belonging.

Some churches offer an optional intergenerational Sunday school class for whole families or a four-to-six-week period during the summer when the congregation is divided into extended families or tribes for midweek activities. A mission trip or a community service project might be planned for families or for a team of teens and adults. All ages can take part in a church workday. When planning such events, consider making them intergenerational, encourage the participation of all age groups, and be sure that there are appropriate tasks for all.

In addition to periodic intergenerational events, people need to belong to an intergenerational community so that over time they can get to know one another and to value each other deeply. Some church leaders fear that cliques will form and destroy the unity of a church if people are clustered in groups for an extended period of time. Although that concern has some legitimacy, the greater risk is that people will never experience a true sense of belonging, support, and accountability in a faith community unless they connect long term with a small group.

Ongoing small groups, whether home-based groups or a Sunday school class, can be encouraged to build in regular time together with a mix of generations. Regular events for the whole family of group members can provide them with an extended family. The option of forming groups for two or three generations of adults can be provided, or a few middle-aged or older adults can be encouraged to participate in a young adult class if the young adults desire that contact. Young families can be encouraged to adopt grandparents, aunts, or uncles from the church family and older adults to adopt children and grand-children. Those who desire a mentoring relationship can be identi-fied and helped to make connections. The church can be the extended family if leaders prayerfully and intentionally guide in that direction.

Support for Families

Parents who desire a family in which they and their children can develop a Christian worldview and who, in response to Christ's call, choose not to make materialism and self-fulfillment their ultimate val-ues but choose to let love for God and others guide their living must walk against the crowd. Worthy intentions to live simply and to share our resources with the poor, to participate in racial reconciliation, or to simplify life so that there is quality time for family and others often evaporate in the heat of social pressure when a lone family strives to be different. The support of others with a similar vision supplies strength necessary for countercultural living. In the faith community of the church or a smaller group within the church, parents can explore what it means to live out the principles of Jesus' teaching in every area of life. Together they can identify the guidelines they believe God would have them set for their family and encourage and hold one another accountable for living by those guidelines. Children in these radical Christian families benefit greatly from a community of friends whose families hold common values.

Serving Together

Wholehearted followers of Jesus are responsive to the needs of those around them. Jesus declared that he "came not to be served but to serve" (Mark 10:45), and in his parable of the last judgment rewarded those who had freely served others without thinking about serving Christ or doing their Christian duty (Matt. 25:31–40). As we become more Christlike, service to others plays an increasing role in our lives and over time shifts from being something a Christian should do to being a way of life. That process can begin during childhood as children have opportunities, through their families and their faith community, to participate in caring and in serving. Many families and Sunday school classes involve children in supporting a child from a developing nation through a monthly contribution for food, education, and medical care. As boys and girls learn about the children they support, regularly pray for them, and contribute financially, they are participating in the worldwide community of faith and are learning the joy of serving.

Children may be the ones to lead adults into expressions of servanthood. One Wednesday evening a little girl arrived at Kids Club barefoot because she had no shoes. Audrey had plenty of shoes and, when her mother suggested it, willingly gave a pair to the little girl. That one act of giving did not satisfy Audrey. She realized several of the children coming to Kids Club needed clothing. "We have an extra room at church and lots of clothes that we don't wear. Why don't we set up a Clothes Closet where people can come to get the shoes and clothes they need?" Adults took ten-year-old Audrey's suggestion seriously, let her have the empty room for her Clothes Closet, and helped her announce the new ministry. The church responded, and within a few weeks the room was overflowing with good used clothing.

Audrey's loving family took time to serve, and her caring spirit began to form there. Her faith community fanned the spark of sensitive responsiveness in her by valuing her idea and participating with her in her ministry. At ten she experienced the joy of service and discovered what the community of faith could do by working together.

THE MASTER STORY

A trail map is basic equipment for hikers whether they explore trails in a nearby nature preserve or spend a week backpacking in a national forest. I can follow the simple map at the nature preserve with confidence, but on the more complex trails of the national forest, I do not trust my trail map reading skills. On one of my hikes, I trusted someone else to lead the way and would have been hopelessly lost if she had not read the map correctly.

On the spiritual journey we might compare the master story of our faith to the trail map. Many people may feel confident following the story map in familiar territory or may trust others who know the story well to lead the way, but many are not equipped to interpret the story and receive guidance from it for new situations. Knowing the faith master story and how to interpret it is critical to the spiritual journey; it may be a life and death issue.

A Story for All Ages

Those ministering with children in the church usually assume that telling Bible stories is one of their major responsibilities and most effective teaching methods. When I was a child, my teachers told me the stories of Scripture, but Sunday school was not the only place where I heard them. Every night before we went to sleep, my mother read to us a story from our Bible storybook. Night after night the master story unfolded for us, without a week between the stories for us to forget the last episode. One of the best gifts we can give our children is the biblical master story, and children are most likely to make the story their own when church and home work together at the task.

However, children are not the only ones who need to learn the stories of Scripture. Many children become adolescents and adults without having learned the master story. Some adults with whom our churches minister have not heard many of the stories. In groups and classes for adults we often try to give them an understanding of the Christian faith by teaching the basic beliefs—the theological system—of our church. We lead them in discussing how Christians should respond to life situations and issues, but seldom do we tell them the faith story.

Apparently many assume that learning stories is just for children and that adults grasp the deep realities of faith best when they are packaged in well-crafted statements about God. But God chose to be revealed through the stories of the Bible, stories of God actively relating to people, and stories of God becoming flesh and living among those people. To know God we must know the stories of God, not just the stories of how we experience God today, as important as they are, but the stories of God active throughout history—the master story of the Christian faith. Unless our understanding of God grows out of that master story, it is more a philosophy than a biblical theology. No one is ever too old to benefit from learning the faith stories and reflecting on them.

Earlier we noted the system of religious practices that God directed Moses to establish for the Hebrew people. Every year in the celebration of the Passover the Israelites reenacted the story of how God delivered them from slavery. They were to tell the story again and again to their children each time they asked why the Hebrews were different from those living around them. Faithfully telling the story to the children kept adults from forgetting it and brought it back to mind for their further reflection and understanding.

Telling or reading Bible stories to children is still one of the best ways for adults to learn the stories for themselves. Young parents who take seriously their responsibility to give their children the stories of the faith will benefit greatly as they enter the stories with their children and meet God there. Adult education in the church should also offer the opportunity for people to learn the stories. Basic beliefs will carry the most meaning for new Christians when they discover the beliefs in the stories of Scripture where a particular reality of God can be seen.

Learning the Whole Story

Examining isolated stories, however, can lead to misunderstanding when interpreted without knowing the flow of the master story. Christian education must provide children, youth, and adults with opportunities to learn and revisit the whole story. Too often Christian teachers focus on New Testament stories, ignoring most of the Old Testament. Frequently, efforts to introduce people to Christianity begin by presenting the stories of Jesus. The birth, life, death, and resurrection of Jesus is at the heart of the gospel; however, without the Old Testament part of the story, there is no reason for Christ's redemptive work.

The Christian master story begins with a Creator God who created humans in his own image and declared them very good. The humans, created with the power of choice, soon chose to disobey God and suffered the consequences of their willful action—death of their totally open, trusting relationship with God, and distortion of their relationship with one another. Wonder of wonders, God did not abandon these rebellious children but, even while explaining the results of their actions, promised to destroy the one who had drawn them into sin (Genesis 1–3).

In the Old Testament we see God choosing Abraham's family to become the people of God so that through them the whole world would be blessed (Gen. 12:2–3). Others are blessed as they see how God related to people in grace, patience, and tough love, and as they see that the blessing of salvation comes through Jesus, the Son of God and a descendant of Abraham. In the light of the Old Testament story, the death and resurrection of Jesus has meaning as we see our gracious God's action to destroy the power of sin and to make it possible again for human beings to come into a completely open, trusting relationship with God.

In our churches and homes do we tell the whole master story? As parents read through the Bible storybook, they give their children the whole story. Some Sunday school curriculum resources try to give children the whole story, but unfortunately many children attend irregularly, missing many of the stories. Overviews of the master story need to be built into the Christian education ministries of the church at several points so people have the opportunity to learn the full story as children, youth, and adults. Children's worship, designed to follow the church year, can lead boys and girls through the flow of the biblical story. By retracing the path of the story each of the three or four years when children have their own worship time, they can make the outline of the master story their own.[8] An overview of the story might also be built into confirmation or membership classes for teenagers and into a quarter of their Sunday school studies.

New seminary students are often asked to tell the story of how they decided to attend seminary, and in many of those stories I hear a common component. They got involved in a small-group Bible study where they committed themselves to intensive study. Over a nine-month period they studied the Bible on their own and met with their group weekly to discuss the meaning of the Scriptures and how they applied to their lives. They studied through the Bible in nine months, and their lives were transformed.[9] Many of these are second-career adults who have sold prosperous businesses and become students in midlife to prepare for the ministry. Their whole worldview changed when they discovered the Christian master story—the whole story.

The story is crucial to spiritual formation at all ages. Learning and reflecting on the master story never grows stale, because each time we come to it from a different place on our journey, we discover new insights about God and ourselves. The Bible gives us one story for all generations to share. As we learn and reflect on it together, we each benefit from the discoveries of others and are bonded together in community by our shared master story.

The Value of Other Stories

Other stories can also enrich the lives of children and adults as they share them together. One characteristic of quality children's literature is that the story fascinates the child and provides insight and humor for the adult as well. Authors such as C. S. Lewis in *The Chronicles of Narnia*[10] and David and Karen Mains in *Tales of the Kingdom*[11] have written powerful metaphors of the Christian master story and life. Metaphors, says N. T. Wright, bring "two sets of ideas close together, close enough for a spark to jump, but not too close, so that the spark, in jumping, illuminates for a moment the whole area around."[12]

Children can identify with characters in such stories and can sense the ugliness of evil and the beauty of good. The adults who read the stories to the children see human weakness and goodness and God's grace and power in a new light, which may rekindle their wonder at God's love.

Once children learn to read, parents and teachers may send them off on their own to enjoy their books. This opens to the young reader the worlds of many more books, but something is missing. When adults and children read aloud together, they share the experiences of the characters in the story, journeying with them and learning from them. With each shared experience, relationships are enriched between those who entered the story together.

One evening many years ago our whole family sat and cried together as my father read aloud the last chapter of *Uncle Tom's Cabin*. If I had read that chapter alone, I might have remembered the story, but the memory would not have connected with the warmth of family togetherness. This is not to say that children should not be encouraged to read on their own, but rather, it is to encourage parents and teachers to read aloud regularly to children and journey with them into the metaphors that shed light on all our lives. In that process our relationships with each other are also enriched.

In contemporary culture many stories are delivered by way of movies, television, or videos. Quality stories portrayed on the screen can provide children with significant insights and leave a lasting impression on them. As with the books discussed above, the value of stories is enhanced when viewed as a family and talked about together and when relational communication is combined with the viewing. Adults who care about the spiritual formation of children will be on the lookout for life-forming stories whether in books, videos, or movies. In the finding and sharing of those stories, both children and adults benefit.

Entering Stories through Imagination

Imagination is often considered to be something children use in play and then discard when they become adults and put away childish things. We are therefore not surprised to learn that children use their imagination to enter stories, to experience them, and even to meet God there, but few adults think of using their imagination to meet God. However, following the lead of children could enrich the spiritual walk for adults.

So often we read the printed words on the pages of our Bibles and think, oh yes, I know that story. But what would we discover if we took the time to enter the story and imagine ourselves there, standing on the roadside, for example, on the first Palm Sunday? What would we see in Jesus' eyes as he looked over the crowd? How would the disciples be acting, and what would they be thinking? Where would we be? Would we be as close as we could get to the Lord, shouting praises, or would we be hanging back, quietly watching? Exercising our imagination in Bible study can make the characters of the story come alive for us and may even help us sense the reality of God's love and grace in new ways.

As we prepare to tell Bible stories to children, we need to dust off our imagination and enter the story as the children will, to see the events and to feel the drama as the story unfolds. When we have been there in our imagination, the story becomes real to us and comes alive for the children as we tell it. The way in which we present the stories of Scripture may influence the attitudes of children toward the Bible. If they are bored by our stories, they will assume the Bible is boring and will want to spend no more time than they must learning about it. But if the stories have become real to us, the children will sense our excitement and join us, through their imaginations, in the story. They will learn to love the God they meet there and will want to return again and again. Imagination brings stories to life for both children and adults.

DYNAMIC CHANGE ON THE JOURNEY

A familiar voice greeted me from the answering machine. "Hi, *Great* Aunt Cathy. This is *Aunt* Tammy calling." Erika had joined our family on the life journey bringing a new role for Tammy and for me. Now Tammy could experience the joys of being an aunt—joys that have been mine since her birth—and I would discover what it means to be a great aunt.

Tammy is no longer the little girl for whom I made doll clothes or to whom I read Santa Mouse stories. She is now the young woman with whom I go to see *Les Miserables* and with whom I share the feelings the musical stirred within us. She is also the young woman whose eyes sparkle as she tells me of talking with a young soldier about God's grace and forgiveness. Our relationship is dynamic and changing as we grow and move into new phases of our lives. Walking with Tammy through her childhood brought me great pleasure, and now I find joy in being adult friends, still on the journey together, looking forward to walking with our new little niece.

While our family enjoyed Erika during her first Christmas with us, we also worked out the plans for moving our father into a retirement home. The one who had cared for us and had launched us into productive lives now needed his children to make decisions and to manage business details for him. These roles were new to us and difficult, both for father and children, but how thankful we were that we walked that section of the road together. The newest member of the family blessed us all as her smiles sparked love and joy in our hearts so that grief did not rule. Even in a time touched by sadness, Erika could still see in the eyes of a whole family that she was loved.

Life is dynamic, changing, and challenging as we journey together. Just when we think we have mastered what is expected of us, relationships change, new persons join us on the journey, or circumstances call for untried roles. Most of us are more comfortable with the known and want to feel confident in our knowledge and abilities before taking on new challenges. But life does not remain static or wait for us to get ready. We can never be fully prepared for what we will face around the next bend in the road. We must learn, grow, and change in the process of living and relating to one another.

Christians, however, can take comfort in knowing that they have a guide on the journey—the Spirit of God. The responsibility of sharing our life-walk with others need not weigh us down and make us anxious, because God is with us. All God asks of us is trusting availability, and the Spirit of God will work within us and within those walking with us, forming and transforming us all.

Children and adults are pilgrims together on the life-walk with God working in and through the flow of normal, changing lives and relationships. By understanding how children are developing and what influences that development, adults are better prepared to enhance the journey for children, to relax and enjoy the journey with them. And God blesses adults and enhances our formation through the little ones with whom we walk.

NOTES

CHAPTER 1: PREPARING FOR THE JOURNEY

1. Some professional educators in the field of religion prefer to be positioned in the broader field that includes all religions and, thus, refer to themselves as *religious educators*. Others place themselves within the Christian faith and choose the designation *Christian educators*. *Religious educators* is used here because many leaders in the social-science approach would refer to themselves in this way.

2. James Michael Lee strongly advocates the social-science approach to religious instruction and addresses the danger of overspiritualizing religious education in *The Shape of Religious Instruction* (Dayton, Ohio: Pflaum, 1971), 191, 196, 209.

3. Melvin Dieter served for many years on the faculty of Asbury Theological Seminary as professor of church history and historical theology. Dieter's model is an adaptation of the Wesley Quadrilateral, the name given to the method for doing theology that scholars, particularly Albert Outler, have identified in the work of John Wesley. Some have presented the Quadrilateral in a way that makes Scripture equal with tradition, reason, and experience. I believe Dieter's model, which places Scripture as the heart or core of theology, is a more accurate representation of Wesley. Wesley proclaimed that he was a man of one book, the Bible, yet in forming his theology he brought Scripture into interaction with tradition, reason, and experience. Wesley read widely the writings of the early church and valued the Christian tradition. He believed in what he called "plundering the Egyptians"—studying the various fields of knowledge in his day such as medicine

and literature, taking truth and effective methods from any source, and using them for the glory of God. He respected the power of reason to recognize truth when it was presented while acknowledging that reason alone was not sufficient to bring salvation. Wesley was a student of human experience. He observed what God was doing in the hearts and lives of those awakened to God through the Methodist revival, and he continued to study the Word of God. Out of this process, his theology and practice of ministry formed, matured, and was refined. Even though all these sources were influential, Scripture always held primacy.

4. N. T. Wright provides a most helpful discussion of biblical interpretation in *The New Testament and the People of God* (Minneapolis: Fortress Press, 1992), 3–144.

5. Robert Mulholland defines *spiritual formation* as "a process of being conformed to the image of Christ for the sake of others" in *Invitation to a Journey: A Road Map for Spiritual Formation* (Downers Grove, Ill.: InterVarsity Press, 1993), 12. Lawrence Richards says, "Christian spirituality is living a human life in this world in union with God" in *A Practical Theology of Spirituality* (Grand Rapids: Zondervan, 1987), 50.

6. William O. Paulsell, *Taste and See: A Personal Guide to the Spiritual Life* (Nashville: The Upper Room, 1976), 2.

7. James Michael Lee, ed., *The Spirituality of the Religious Educator* (Birmingham, Ala.: Religious Education Press, 1985), 7.

8. John J. Gleason Jr., *Growing Up to God: Eight Steps in Religious Development* (Nashville: Abingdon Press, 1975), 21.

9. John Wesley talked about the way of salvation as a way of grace. Along that way, from birth to death, God offers us prevenient, converting, and sanctifying grace. Prevenient grace is the grace that goes before conversion, giving a dawning awareness of God and preparing us to receive converting grace, the forgiveness of sin, and new life in Christ. Sanctifying grace makes it possible for us, by the power of God's Spirit, to become more and more Christlike.

10. W. W. Meissner, *Life and Faith: Psychological Perspectives on Religious Experience* (Washington, D.C.: Georgetown University Press, 1987), 23, 58–74.

CHAPTER 2: CHILDREN IN THE BIBLE

1. James E. Reed and Ronnie Prevost, *A History of Christian Education* (Nashville: Broadman and Holman, 1993), 49.

2. James W. Fowler, *Stages of Faith: The Psychology of Human Development and the Quest for Meaning* (San Francisco: Harper & Row, 1981), 14.

3. Notes in *The Wesley Bible* (Nashville: Thomas Nelson, 1990), 263.

4. Ibid., 250.

5. Abraham Z. Idelsohn, *The Ceremonies of Judaism* (Cincinnati: National Federation of Temple Brotherhoods, 1930), 40–43.

6. Reed and Prevost, *Christian Education*, 47–48.

7. Read about the tabernacle in Exodus 26–27, 30, 40; Numbers 4:5–15.

8. This is the count from the New Revised Standard Version.

9. One example of the commentaries that believe Jesus is not referring to children in Matthew 18:5–14 is *The Wycliffe Bible Commentary*, ed. Charles F. Pfeiffer and Everett F. Harrison (Chicago: Moody, 1962), 961.

10. Lawrence O. Richards, *Children's Ministry, Nurturing Faith within the Family of God* (Grand Rapids: Zondervan, 1983), 76.

11. John H. Westerhoff III, *Will Our Children Have Faith?* (New York: Seabury Press, 1976), 23.

12. Robert D. Hess, "Experts and Amateurs: Some Unintended Consequences of Parent Education," in *Parenting in a Multicultural Society*, ed. Mario D. Fantini and René Cardenas (New York: Longman, 1980), 150, 155.

13. Ibid., 156–57.

14. Richards, *Children's Ministry*, 191.

15. Ibid., 76.

CHAPTER 3: FOUNDATIONS FOR FAITH

1. Erik H. Erikson, *Childhood and Society* (New York: W. W. Norton, 1985), 18, 114.

2. Carol K. Sigelman and David R. Shaffer, *Life-Span Human Development*, 2d ed. (Pacific Grove, Calif.: Brooks/Cole Publishing, 1995), 32.

3. Ibid., 269.

4. Erikson, *Childhood and Society*, 34–36.

5. Ibid., 34.

6. Barbara M. Newman and Philip R. Newman, *Development through Life: A Psychosocial Approach*, 6th ed. (Pacific Grove, Calif.: Brooks/Cole Publishing, 1995), 49; and James W. Fowler, *Stages of Faith: The Psychology of Human Development and the Quest for Meaning* (San Francisco: Harper & Row, 1981), 48.

7. Newman and Newman, *Development through Life*, 52.

8. Fowler, *Stages of Faith*, 50–51; and Sigelman and Shaffer, *Life-Span Human Development*, 269.

9. Newman and Newman, *Development through Life*, 49, 51.

10. Ibid., 50–51.

11. Erikson, *Childhood and Society*, 274.

12. Ibid., 249.

13. Ibid., 247–51; see also Fowler, *Stages of Faith*, 55.

14. Erikson, *Childhood and Society*, 249.

15. Ibid., 250.

16. Newman and Newman, *Development through Life*, 229.

17. Fowler, *Stages of Faith*, 55.

18. Erikson, *Childhood and Society*, 72.

19. Ibid., 74.

20. Ibid., 75–76.

21. Ibid., 247.

22. Ibid., 274.

23. Iris V. Cully, *Christian Child Development* (San Francisco: Harper & Row, 1979), 5.

24. Erikson, *Childhood and Society*, 82.

25. Newman and Newman, *Development through Life*, 278.

26. Erikson, *Childhood and Society*, 82–83.

27. Ibid., 252.

28. Ibid.

29. Erik H. Erikson, *Insight and Responsibility* (New York: W. W. Norton, 1964), 119.

30. Cully, *Child Development*, 7.

31. Erikson, *Childhood and Society*, 253–54.

32. Erikson, *Insight and Responsibility*, 119.

33. Erikson, *Childhood and Society*, 254.

34. Ibid., 255.

35. Newman and Newman, *Development through Life*, 334.

36. Erik H. Erikson, *Identity Youth and Crisis* (New York: W. W. Norton, 1968), 115.

37. Erikson, *Childhood and Society*, 258.

38. Erikson, *Identity Youth and Crisis*, 119.

39. Erikson, *Insight and Responsibility*, 121–22.

40. Erikson, *Childhood and Society*, 257; and Erikson, *Identity Youth and Crisis*, 119–20.

41. Newman and Newman, *Development through Life*, 335, 337.

42. Erikson, *Childhood and Society*, 149.

43. Ibid., 95.

44. Erikson, *Identity Youth and Crisis*, 121.

45. Erikson, *Insight and Responsibility*, 120.

46. Newman and Newman, *Development through Life*, 338–39.

47. Erikson, *Insight and Responsibility*, 122.

48. Newman and Newman, *Development through Life*, 389.

49. Erikson, *Childhood and Society*, 259.

50. Newman and Newman, *Development through Life*, 388–89.

51. Erikson, *Identity Youth and Crisis*, 127, 123–24.

52. Ibid., 123; and Erikson, *Childhood and Society*, 258–60.

53. Erikson, *Identity Youth and Crisis*, 124–25.

54. Newman and Newman, *Development through Life*, 387–88.

55. Erikson, *Childhood and Society*, 260–61.

56. Erikson, *Identity Youth and Crisis*, 126; and Fowler, *Stages of Faith*, 67.

57. Erikson, *Childhood and Society*, 404.

58. David Seamands, *Healing Grace: Let God Free You from the Performance Trap* (Wheaton: Victor, 1988), 46.

59. William Mahedy and Janet Bernardi, *A Generation Alone: Xers Making a Place in the World* (Downers Grove, Ill.: InterVarsity Press, 1994). I have drawn from this source for the information on Generation X.

60. Erikson, *Childhood and Society*, 269.

Chapter 4: Young Learners in Action

1. David Elkind, *Children and Adolescents: Interpretive Essays on Jean Piaget*, 2d ed. (New York: Oxford University Press, 1974), 14.

2. Ibid., 108.

3. Ibid., 20.

4. Jean Piaget and Barbel Inhelder, *The Psychology of the Child* (New York: Basic Books, 1969), 6.

5. Jean Piaget, *Six Psychological Studies* (New York: Random House, 1967), 6–7, 122–25.

6. Ibid., 6.

7. Piaget and Inhelder, *Psychology*, 10–11.

8. Piaget, *Studies*, 79.

9. Piaget and Inhelder, *Psychology*, 13.

10. Piaget, *Studies*, 29.

11. Ibid., 20–21.

12. Ibid., 30.

13. Ibid.

14. Piaget and Inhelder, *Psychology*, 93–94.

15. Ibid.

16. Elkind, *Children and Adolescents*, 25, 52.

17. Piaget, *Studies*, 79–80; and Piaget and Inhelder, *Psychology*, 77–78, 82.

18. Piaget, *Studies*, 24–25.

19. Elkind, *Children and Adolescents*, 33–34, 37.

20. Piaget, *Studies*, 38–40.

21. Ibid., 41, 48; and Piaget and Inhelder, *Psychology*, 96.

22. Piaget and Inhelder, *Psychology*, 100.

23. Piaget, *Studies*, 46.

24. Ibid., 46–47.

25. Elkind, *Children and Adolescents*, 47–48.

26. Piaget and Inhelder, *Psychology*, 128–29.

27. Piaget, *Studies*, 125.

28. Ibid., 61.

29. Piaget and Inhelder, *Psychology*, 132.

30. Piaget, *Studies*, 61, 63.

31. For information on learning styles and Myers/Briggs, see Bernice McCarthy, *The 4MAT System* (Barington, Ill.: EXCEL, 1987).

32. Piaget, *Studies*, 103, 127.

33. Jean Piaget, "Piaget's Theory," in *Carmichael's Manual of Child Psychology*, ed. Paul H. Mussen, 3d ed. (New York: John Wiley & Sons, 1970), 719–20.

34. Ibid., 720–21.

35. Ibid., 721.

36. John H. Flavell, *The Developmental Psychology of Jean Piaget* (New York: Van Nostrand Reinhold, 1963), 369.

37. This is the view of behaviorists such as B. F. Skinner.

38. Piaget, "Theory," 721.

39. Ibid., 726.

40. Piaget, *Studies*, 101.

41. Elkind, *Children and Adolescents*, 122–23, 126.

42. Ibid., 136.

43. Ibid., 53.

44. Ibid., 137.

45. Ibid., 155.

46. Ibid., 108.

CHAPTER 5: THE CHILD'S VIEW ON RIGHT AND WRONG

1. Lawrence Kohlberg, "My Personal Search for Universal Morality," in *The Kohlberg Legacy for the Helping Professions*, Lisa Kuhmerker (Birmingham, Ala.: R.E.P. Books, 1991), 15.

2. Lawrence Kohlberg, "Moral Education in the Schools: A Developmental View," in *Curriculum and the Cultural Revolution*, ed. David E. Purpel and Maurice Blanger (Berkeley: McCutchan, 1972), 456. Kohlberg reports on the 1928–30 study of Hartshorne and May and notes that more recent research has confirmed their findings.

3. Jean Piaget, *Six Psychological Studies* (New York: Vintage Books, 1967), 36.

4. Lawrence Kohlberg, *The Philosophy of Moral Development: Essays on Moral Development*, vol. 1 (San Francisco: Harper & Row, 1981), 172.

5. Lawrence Kohlberg, *The Psychology of Moral Development: Essays on Moral Development*, vol. 2 (San Francisco: Harper & Row, 1984), 172. Kohlberg also notes that often adolescents and adults involved in criminal activity use stage 2 moral reasoning.

6. Ibid., 172–73.

7. Jean Piaget, *The Moral Judgment of the Child* (New York: The Free Press, 1965), 27.

8. Ibid.

9.Lawrence Kohlberg, "Stages and Sequence: The Cognitive-Developmental Approach to Socialization," in *Handbook of Socialization Theory and Research*, ed. David A. Goslin (Chicago: Rand McNally, 1969), 376.

10. Kohlberg, *Philosophy*, 17.

11. Ibid., 409; Kohlberg, *Psychology*, 624; and Piaget, *Studies*, 36–37.

12. Piaget, *Moral Judgment*, 122–25.

13. Piaget, *Studies*, 37.

14. Piaget, *Moral Judgment*, 89.

15. Kohlberg, *Philosophy*, 409.

16. Ibid., 17; and Piaget, *Studies*, 36.

17. Jean Piaget and Barbel Inhelder, *The Psychology of the Child* (New York: Basic Books, 1969), 124.

18. Kohlberg, *Philosophy*, 121.

19. Kohlberg, "Stages and Sequence," 381.

20. Ibid., 379.

21. Ibid.

22. Kohlberg, *Psychology*, 173–77.

23. Kohlberg, *Philosophy*, 409.

24. Ibid., 409–10; and Kohlberg, *Psychology*, 174.

25. Piaget, *Studies*, 36–37.

26. Kohlberg, "Moral Education," 461.

27. Ibid.

28. Kohlberg, *Psychology*, 624–25.

29. Piaget, *Studies*, 57.

30. Kohlberg, *Psychology*, 625.

31. Kohlberg, *Philosophy*, 148.

32. Kohlberg, *Psychology*, 172.

33. Ibid., 174.

34. Ibid., 175, 178.

35. Ibid., 174.

36. Ibid., 175.

37. Ibid., 174, 629; Kohlberg, *Philosophy*, 121; and Kohlberg, "Moral Education," 460.

38. Kohlberg, *Psychology*, 175; Kohlberg, "Moral Education," 460; Kohlberg, "Stages and Sequence," 381; and Kohlberg, *Philosophy*, 18.

39. Kohlberg, *Philosophy*, 18; and Kohlberg, "Stages and Sequence," 380.

40. Kohlberg, "Stages and Sequence," 380.

41. Kohlberg, *Philosophy*, 410.

42. Ibid., 411.

43. Ibid., 119.

44. Piaget, *Studies*, 38, 55.

45. Kohlberg, *Philosophy*, 119, 411.

46. Ibid., 149.

47. Kohlberg, *Psychology*, 631.

48. Lyn Mikel Brown and Carol Gilligan, *Meeting at the Crossroads: Women's Psychology and Girls' Development* (Cambridge, Mass.: Harvard University Press, 1992), 216–32.

49. Kohlberg, *Psychology*, 172.

50. Ibid., 173, 175–76.

51. Ibid., 176; and Kohlberg, *Philosophy*, 411.

52. Kohlberg, *Psychology*, 176.

53. Ibid., 175.

54. Kohlberg, *Philosophy*, 121–22; and Kohlberg, "Moral Education," 460.

55. Kohlberg, *Psychology*, 176; and Kohlberg, "Stages and Sequence," 382.

56. Kohlberg, "Stages and Sequence," 380.

57. Ibid.

58. Ibid., 376; and Kohlberg, *Psychology*, 175.

59. Kohlberg, *Psychology*, 636.

60. Kohlberg, *Philosophy*, 119.

61. Ibid., 120.

62. Kohlberg, *Psychology*, 623, 635–36.

63. Ibid., 636–37.

64. Ibid., 202.

65. Ibid., 74.

66. Ibid., 155.

67. Ibid., 121.

68. Kohlberg, *Philosophy*, 142.

69. Kohlberg, *Psychology*, 74.

70. Ibid., 76.

71. Ibid.

72. Ibid., 76–77, 199–200.

73. Ibid., 201; and Kohlberg, *Philosophy*, 144.

74. Kohlberg, "Personal Search," 17.

75. Kohlberg, *Psychology*, 80.

76. Ibid., 198.

77. Kohlberg, "Moral Education," 473.

78. Ibid.; and Kohlberg, *Psychology*, 79–80.

79. Kohlberg, "Moral Education," 474.

80. Ibid., 474–75.

81. Kohlberg, *Philosophy*, 146.

82. Kohlberg, *Psychology*, 80–81.

83. Kohlberg, "Moral Education," 459, 476.

84. Kohlberg, *Psychology*, 558–60.

85. Ibid., 71.

86. Piaget, *Studies*, 60.

87. Kohlberg, *Philosophy*, 321–22, 336.

88. Kohlberg, *Psychology*, 536–37.

89. Robert Coles, *The Moral Life of Children* (Boston: Houghton Mifflin, 1986), 4, 9–11, 250.

90. Ibid., 21, 23, 25, 29.

91. Ibid., 103–5, 118–120, 129.

92. Ibid., 34, 133.

93. Ibid., 23–24.

94. Ibid., 135.

CHAPTER 6: KNOWING GOD IN CHILDHOOD

1. Walter Wangerin Jr., *Little Lamb, Who Made Thee? A Book about Children and Parents* (Grand Rapids: Zondervan, 1993), 33. This is a marvelous book of stories, which should be required reading for all parents and Christian educators.

2. Ronald Goldman is one such religious educator who has influenced many others. For an understanding of his research and conclusions, see *Religious Thinking from Childhood to Adolescence* (London: Routledge and Kegan Paul, 1964), and *Readiness for Religion* (London: Routledge and Kegan Paul, 1965).

3. Sofia Cavalletti, *The Religious Potential of the Child: The Description of an Experience with Children from Ages Three to Six*, trans. Patricia M. Coulter and Julie M. Coulter (New York: Paulist Press, 1983), 31–32.

4. Edward Robinson, *The Original Vision: A Study of the Religious Experience of Childhood* (Oxford: The Religious Experience Research Unit, Manchester College, 1977), 11.

5. Ana-Maria Rizzuto, *The Birth of the Living God: A Psychoanalytic Study* (Chicago and London: University of Chicago Press, 1979), 7, 178.

6. Ibid., 44–45.

7. Ibid., 7.

8. Ibid.

9. Ibid., 182–83.

10. Ibid., 122, 187.

11. Ibid., 182–83.

12. Ibid., 76–77, 83, 190.

13. Ibid., 184, 193, 209.

14. Ibid., 186; and James W. Fowler, "Strength for the Journey: Early Childhood Development in Selfhood and Faith," in *Faith Development in Early Childhood*, ed. Doris A. Blazer (Kansas City, Mo.: Sheed and Ward, 1989), 30.

15. Rizzuto, *Living God*, 46.

16. Ibid., 194.

17. Ibid., 45, 179.

18. Ibid., 52, 90.

19. Ibid., 8.

20. Ibid., 203.

21. Ibid., 9–10.

22. Polly Berrien Berends, *Gently Lead: How to Teach Your Children about God While Finding Out for Yourself* (New York: HarperCollins, 1991), 88.

23. Sonja M. Stewart and Jerome W. Berryman, *Young Children and Worship* (Louisville: Westminster/John Knox Press, 1989), 105.

24. Berends, *Gently Lead*, 8–9.

25. Robert Coles, *The Spiritual Life of Children* (Boston: Houghton Mifflin, 1990), xiii.

26. Ibid., 36. Coles's findings come from in-depth conversations with children. He interviewed most of the five hundred children at least five times and over one hundred of them twenty-five or more times. He talked repeatedly with some of the children over a full year and with others during a two-year span of time.

27. Ibid., 23, 25, 37, 100, 168–69, 294.

28. Ibid., 121.

29. Ibid., 192–93, 207–9.

30. Ibid., 204–5.

31. Ibid., 118.

32. Ibid., 90, 76.

33. Ibid., 94.

34. Ibid., 95.

35. Ibid., 48–49.

36. Ibid., 40.

37. Ibid., 64, 170.

CHAPTER 7: GROWING IN FAITH

1. Acts 2:25–26; Romans 3:22, 26; Galatians 2:16; Ephesians 1:15; Philippians 3:9; and Colossians 1:4, to mention only a few.

2. V. Bailey Gillespie, *The Experience of Faith* (Birmingham, Ala.: Religious Education Press, 1988), 24.

3. James W. Fowler, *Weaving the New Creation: Stages of Faith and the Public Church* (New York: HarperCollins, 1991), 100–101.

4. This thought comes from a sermon by Dr. Robert Mulholland, "The Weaned Child at Its Mother's Breast," Asbury Theological Seminary Chapel, Wilmore, Ky., 8 February 1994.

5. N. T. Wright, *The New Testament and the People of God* (Minneapolis: Fortress Press, 1992), 97–98, 123, 132–33. Wright briefly outlines his master story: "I find myself driven, both from my study of the New Testament and from a wide variety of other factors which contribute to my being who I am, to tell a story about reality which runs something like this. Reality as we know it is the result of a creator [G]od bringing into being a world that is other than himself, and yet which is full of his glory. It was always the intent of this [G]od that creation should one day be flooded with his own life, in a way for which it was prepared from the beginning. As part of the means to this end, the creator brought into being a creature which, by bearing the creator's image, would bring wise and loving care to bear upon the creation. By a tragic irony, the creature in question rebelled against this intention. But the creator has solved this problem in principle in an entirely appropriate way (acting through Israel and climactically through Jesus, to rescue his creation), and as a result is now moving the creation once more toward its originally intended goal. The implementation of this solution now involves the indwelling of this [G]od within his human creatures and ultimately within the whole creation, transforming it into that for which it was made in the beginning," 97–98.

6. Fowler, *Weaving*, 101.

7. Wright, *People of God*, 117.

8. Fowler, *Weaving*, 102.

9. James W. Fowler, *Faith Development and Pastoral Care* (Philadelphia: Fortress Press, 1987), 57; James W. Fowler, *Stages of Faith* (San Francisco: Harper & Row, 1981), 109; and Fowler, *Weaving*, 100.

10. James W. Fowler, "Strength for the Journey: Early Childhood Development in Selfhood and Faith," in *Faith Development in Early Childhood*, ed. Doris A. Blazer (Kansas City, Mo.: Sheed and Ward, 1989), 7.

11. Fowler, *Stages*, 121.

12. Fowler, *Pastoral Care*, 58; and Fowler, *Stages*, 16–17.

13. Fowler, "Strength," 12–13.

14. Ibid., 14.

15. Fowler, *Weaving*, 103.

16. Fowler, *Stages*, 123.

17. Fowler, *Weaving*, 103.

18. Fowler, "Strength," 35.

19. Ibid., 133.

20. Fowler, *Stages*, 57, 123.

21. Ibid., 24.

22. Ibid., 30.

23. Ibid., 26.

24. Ibid., 132–33.

25. Fowler, *Pastoral Care*, 59; and Fowler, "Strength," 28.

26. Fowler, *Stages*, 129.

27. Ibid., 130–31.

28. Ibid., 130.

29. Ibid., 133.

30. Ibid., 130.

31. Fowler, "Strength," 28.

32. Fowler, *Stages*, 132–34.

33. Ibid., 146–47, 149.

34. Ibid., 136.

35. Ibid., 134–36.

36. Ibid., 138.

37. Ibid., 136.

38. Fowler, *Pastoral Care*, 62–63.

39. Fowler, *Stages*, 139, 144–45, 149; Fowler, *Pastoral Care*, 62; and Fowler, *Weaving*, 106.

40. Fowler, *Stages*, 136.

41. Ibid., 149.

42. Ibid.; and Fowler, *Pastoral Care*, 61.

43. Fowler, *Stages*, 149.

44. Ibid., 150, 152; and Fowler, *Pastoral Care*, 63.

45. Fowler, *Stages*, 151.

46. Ibid., 153–54.

47. Ibid., 156.

48. Fowler, *Pastoral Care*, 65.

49. Fowler, *Weaving*, 108.

50. Ibid., 94.

51. Fowler, *Stages*, 132.

52. Ibid., 114.

CHAPTER 8: SETTING THE STAGE FOR KNOWING GOD

1. Walter Wangerin Jr., *The Orphean Passages: The Drama of Faith* (San Francisco: Harper & Row, 1986), 24–25.

2. Jerome W. Berryman, *Godly Play: A Way of Religious Education* (San Francisco: HarperSanFrancisco, 1991), 148–49. Berryman explores the topic of religious language in pages 144–54.

3. Quoted in Edward Robinson, *The Original Vision: A Study of the Religious Experience of Childhood* (Oxford: The Religious Experience Research Unit, Manchester College, 1977), 12–13.

4. Sofia Cavalletti, *The Religious Potential of the Child: The Description of an Experience with Children from Ages Three to Six* (New York: Paulist Press, 1983), 56.

5. Sonja M. Stewart and Jerome W. Berryman, *Young Children and Worship* (Louisville: Westminster/John Knox Press, 1989). The approach being used and the story are from *Young Children and Worship*. I have written the account of children's worship from my memory of working with the children. However, if you compare my account with *Young Children*, you will find that I use the materials almost verbatim.

6. Syble Towner made this observation in a conversation when she was Minister to Families with Children at College Hill Presbyterian Church in Cincinnati, Ohio.

7. Cavalletti, *Religious Potential*, 15, 13–45, 47.

8. Berryman, *Godly Play*, 60; and Cavalletti, *Religious Potential*, 15, 96.

9. Berryman, *Godly Play*, x; and Cavalletti, *Religious Potential*, 41.

10. Cavalletti, *Religious Potential*, 32.

11. Ibid., 14–15, 170.

12. Ibid., 75, 86, 169.

13. Ibid., 87.

14. Ibid., 153.

15. Ibid., 70.

16. Quoted in Berryman, *Godly Play*, 157.

17. Cavalletti, *Religious Potential*, 48–49, 59; and Berryman, *Godly Play*, 158.

18. Cavalletti, *Religious Potential*, 60.

19. Ibid., 51.

20. Berryman, *Godly Play*, 102.

21. Cavalletti, *Religious Potential*, 52, 57–58.

22. Berryman, *Godly Play*, 44.

23. Ibid., 18, 22, 58, 140.

24. Ibid., 63, 83.

25. Cavalletti, *Religious Potential*, 138–39; see ibid., 62–63.

26. Berryman, *Godly Play*, 63–64.

27. Ibid., 21, 90; and Cavalletti, *Religious Potential*, 53, 69.

28. Berryman, *Godly Play*, 55.

29. Ibid., 85.

30. Cavalletti, *Religious Potential*, 63, 75.

31. Ibid., 76, 140–45.

32. Ibid., 73.

33. Berryman, *Godly Play*, 45, 54.

34. If your church does not allow children to partake of the elements, develop some way of inviting the children to come with their parents for a blessing, and communicate to the children anticipation for the special day when they, too, will be able to join in this special meal. If using the Stewart/Berryman stories, you will have to adjust them to fit the practice of your church.

35. Godly play may be used in more interactive, community building ways than what is described in this chapter. For additional possibilities consult Jerome W. Berryman, *Teaching Godly Play: The Sunday Morning Handbook* (Nashville: Abingdon Press, 1995).

36. If you choose this option, Stewart and Berryman's *Young Children and Worship* provides complete guidance, a full set of stories, patterns, and instructions for making materials.

CHAPTER 9: PILGRIMS TOGETHER ON THE JOURNEY

1. "Evaluating Metaphors of Education," in *With an Eye on the Future: Development and Mission in the 21st Century: Essays in Honor of Ted W. Ward,* ed. Duane Elmer and Lois McKinney (Monrovia, Calif.: MARC, 1996), 48–49.

2. Robert Coles, *The Spiritual Life of Children* (Boston: Houghton Mifflin, 1990), 322–23, 351.

3. Neil Kalter, *Growing Up with Divorce: Helping Your Child Avoid Immediate and Later Emotional Problems* (London: Collier Macmillan, 1990), 1.

4. Catherine Clark Kroeger and James R. Beck, ed., *Women, Abuse, and the Bible: How Scripture Can Be Used to Hurt or to Heal* (Grand Rapids: Baker, 1996). This book alerts the church to the prevalence of abuse in Christian homes and provides insights on how to bring healing.

5. Many of the ideas in this section on the impact of television come from a presentation by Michael Medved on 18 October 1996 at the annual meeting of the North American Professors of Christian Education. Medved has written *Hollywood vs. America* (New York: Harper-Perrennial, 1993).

6. Phyllis Kilbourn, ed., *Children in Crisis: A New Commitment* (Monrovia, Calif.: MARC, 1996), 21, 30, 49. This resource provides a description of conditions faced by children but also points to programs and agencies with whom we might work to make a difference in the lives of the world's poorest and most vulnerable travelers.

7. Check with a local counselor, social worker, or police officer to learn what the law requires in reporting suspected child abuse and the resources that are available to children and their families.

8. The curriculum designed by Stewart and Berryman leads children through the biblical story each year.

9. "Disciple Bible Study," published by the United Methodist Publishing House, is the Bible study many Asbury Theological Seminary students have found life transforming.

10. *The Chronicles of Narnia* is a seven-book set of children's stories by C. S. Lewis (New York: Macmillan, Collier Books, 1950–56). The

three volumes that most closely parallel the Christian master story are *The Lion, the Witch and the Wardrobe* (1950), *The Magician's Nephew* (1955), and *The Last Battle* (1956).

11. David and Karen Mains, *Tales of the Kingdom* (Elgin, Ill.: Chariot Books, 1983).

12. N. T. Wright, *The New Testament and the People of God* (Minneapolis: Fortress Press, 1992), 40.

INDEX

Catherine Stonehouse (Ph.D., Michigan State University) is Orlean Bullard Professor of Christian Education at Asbury Theological Seminary, Wilmore, Kentucky, where she regularly teaches about ministry with children. Her extensive background in curriculum writing and local and denominational church ministry (with the Free Methodist Church of North America) contribute to her passion for and expertise in children's concerns. A contributor to several edited volumes, this is her second book.